Brian -

Freedom is not free
3 Those who would take it.
William W. Smith

A Moment in Time

William W. Smith

As told to Charlotte Smith

With the help of God and true love
the human spirit will triumph
Charlatte E. Smith

Gazelle
P R E S S

Mobile, Alabama

ISBN 978-1-58169-272-3
For Worldwide Distribution
Printed in the U.S.A.

Gazelle Press
P.O. Box 191540 • Mobile, AL 36619
800-367-8203

Cover illustration by Robert Craig,
Curator, All Wars Museum,
Art Director, Illinois Veterans Home—Quincy, Illinois

Table of Contents

Dedication

Charlotte—she has lived with me for 51 years through good times and bad. Someone once said, "Being an EX-POW is like living in an overcoat you can never take off." And that is so true. Charlotte has been there to make the coat lighter and my life easier.

Lisa—the best daughter a man could ever have. Being an EX-POW is not like being everyone else's father, and she was always willing to understand.

Allison—My first born granddaughter is so precious to me. Being an EX-POW is sometimes very difficult for a little child to be around. She never thought it wasn't all right. She thought I was a cool granddad.

Sullivan—She is the second born granddaughter and just as precious to me. Being an EX-POW was so trying some days, but in her eyes I could fix anything. She thought I was great.

These four women accept me just as I am and love me. For this reason...

I DEDICATE THIS BOOK TO THEM

WITH MY LOVE

Special Thanks

To Janice Riley, Joyce Schrage, Donna Wilson, and Morey Taraska who worked so hard to prepare this manuscript for the publisher.

Many, many thanks to Robert Craig for the original drawing for the cover. It is exactly the way my hands felt that long ago day in Korea.

Acknowledgments

Charlotte and I have worked on this project for many hours in the quiet of our home and in the noise of public transportation, a doctor's office, our car, a restaurant, almost any place we have been for the last year.

When we started to write, we talked and cried and talked some more and cried some more. We have tried to go over all the incidents that happened to me. We could not include all of them, so we have tried to include the more interesting ones.

We have never done this kind of project before. It was much more difficult to relive those dark, cold, hungry days of the 1950s than either of us thought it would be, although it has been a rewarding experience.

This book was not intended to be a work of art or a piece of great literature. It is intended to be simply the story of what happened to me and a lot of other POWs:

THOSE WHO RETURNED AND THOSE WHO DID NOT!

Introduction

I never thought I would write a book, so I never wrote anything down while I was in the prison camp or when I first returned home. I have tried to remember the times and places as best as I can.

My memories have dimmed in some ways, yet it is as though my captivity in Korea happened yesterday and not 53 years ago. I remember more about Korea than I do what I had for breakfast this morning.

I really wrote this book for my granddaughters, Allison and Sullivan. Sometimes I have been a little different to live with than most grandfathers. That does not mean I love them any less; it only means I love them more. Along with my daughter Lisa and my wife Charlotte, they are the loves of my life. I thank God I survived to come home and have such a wonderful family.

A Letter to My Granddaughters

Dear Allison and Sullivan,

I hope that, after you read this book, you will understand me better.

You will understand why as little girls you could not jump on the bed without waking me first if I were asleep. That was because I was so frightened I might hit you, even though I love you with all my heart.

You will understand why I open any door a crack, look right and left, before I open it all the way. It is my way of protecting you and the ones I love.

You will understand why I react like I do when a balloon has been burst behind me. It is because of the "Russian Roulette" torture and not because of anything you ever did.

You will understand why some of today's political decisions make me so angry. I am worried we will be in another war like Korea and Iraq. I would never want my great grandsons to have to face what I did. I pray this will not come to pass, and good men will make right decisions.

You will understand why some of the men I met and lived with in Korea are closer to me than my own brother. We shared so much, even life and death.

You will understand how precious you, your mother, and your grandmother are to me. You make my life worth living. You give me a reason to get up in the morning and face another day.

I know in my heart God spared me for a reason when so many men did not return. I do not know what that reason is and may never know. But when I look at the two of you I know you are part of the reason I returned.

When you were little you looked at me with the eyes of a child. Now I want you to look at me with the eyes of young women. I thank the Lord for you and your love every day.

Your Grand Pa,

(Bop)

Chapter 1

In the Beginning

This is my story; every word is true as I remember it. It takes the old proverb that "truth is stranger than fiction" to another level. Truth, in my case, is more terrible than a fictional horror story. I will say to you what I always share when speaking before crowds: If you were telling me this story, I wouldn't believe you. Man's inhumanity to man is incredible.

I was born in Bennettsville, South Carolina, in 1929 and grew up on a farm in Rockingham, North Carolina. I believe this life prepared me for the time later in my life when I would be imprisoned in North Korea. I will not go into details about my younger years, but they gave me what I needed to survive what was probably one of the worst experiences anyone could ever have.

Those were the post-depression years, and money was scarce. I used my sister's birth date as mine (she was three years older than I was) and went to work at an early age. As a consequence, when I turned 15, all my records listed me as three years older. Uncle Sam was drafting young men of that age during World War

II, so I became a prime candidate. As a result of the deception about my age, I was drafted when I was really only 15 years old. I entered the Army on December 23, 1944 at Ft. McFearson in Atlanta, Georgia, and took my basic training at Camp Joseph T. Robertson in Arkansas where I was in the 109th Battalion.

I stayed in the Army until May 9, 1945. At that time I was getting ready to be shipped overseas, but my mother decided to take matters into her own hands. She called my father, who was in the Air Force. He went to his Commanding Officer who contacted my C.O., and I was called to his office.

The C.O. told me, "You are a good soldier. Go home and come back when you are 17." That was exactly what I did. In the meantime, I returned home to Rockingham and worked on the family farm.

Into the Army Again

When I was 17, I reentered the Army at Ft. Bragg, North Carolina, on November 5, 1947. I was then sent to Ft. Jackson, South Carolina, for a two-week refresher course. When I finished the course, I was sent to Camp Stoneman, California. Our company stayed at Stoneman for about a month and left on the USS General Haun for Inchon, Korea, in January or February 1948.

I was with H. Company 6th Div. Inf. (Red Star Div) when we headed to Korea during its occupation at the end of WWII. My Division stayed about nine months in Korea until December 28, 1948. After we left Korea, we went to Sasabo, Japan. I served in the 24th Infantry Division, 34th Inf. Reg. Company, M Camp Mower, while I was in Sasabo, Japan.

One morning in the beginning of June 1950, I asked the company clerk if I wasn't due for rotation to the U.S. and a new assignment. We went to the office, and sure enough, I was ready to go home. He cut my orders, and I shipped out of Yokohama, Japan, on June 23, 1950.

We had been at sea only about two days when North Korea attacked South Korea. All my buddies I had just left in Japan were sent into combat immediately, and I would have been sent too if I had stayed. As it was, there were so many civilians on board our ship that we could not return to Japan, so we continued on to the States.

President Truman froze all troops in June 1950 at the outbreak of the war, so even if you wanted to get out of the Army, you couldn't be discharged. Of course I didn't want out because the Army was going to be my career.

After we docked at Ft. Laughtin in Seattle, Washington, I was given leave and went home to Rockingham for a few days. Afterward I was assigned to Edgewood Arsenal in Maryland. I was in the Second Chemical Mortor Battallion. It was considered to be a "bastard" outfit—that means it belonged to no one else.

At first I did not know anyone in this outfit. Eventually I made a friend in this group, Ray Mendel from Baltimore, Maryland. He would turn out to be the best friend a man could ever have. We became "fox hole" buddies. We ate, slept, fought, rested, wrote letters home, and finally were captured together. In the hell hole of captivity, we also looked after each other, watching each other's backs as best we could.

I think that it was the Lord looking after me that Ray and I were able to stay together throughout the entire ordeal of being POWs. At one point after our capture, it looked like we were going to be separated. When I was being moved to Camp 2 in the summer of 1952 by my captors, I thought I was going alone and said a reluctant good-bye to Ray. Two days later, Ray arrived with several others who had been labeled reactionaries and also segregated from the main camp. We were moved to a new camp, Camp 2 Company 3, where we stayed until our repatriation.

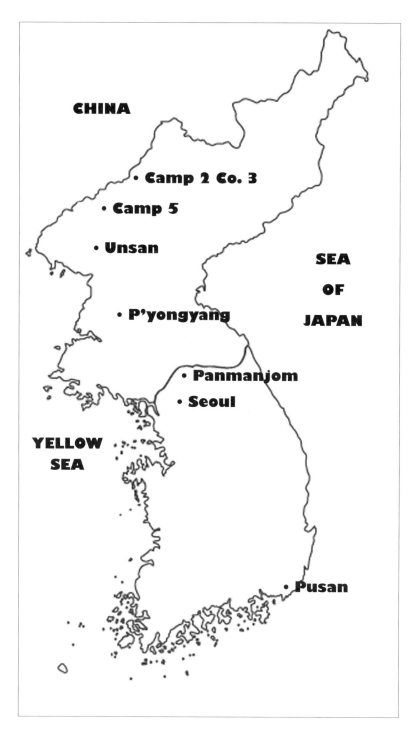

Entering Combat

To the best of my recollection, our outfit landed at the Port of Pusan on the southeast coast of Korea on September 1950 on the USS Shanks and began the long march north. Little did I know I would not be back home for two years, eight months, and ten days, spending almost all of those days in captivity.

I was only in combat 2-1/2 months before I was captured. I did not know when I stepped off the boat in Pusan that my journey would take me to China and almost to the Manchurian border, or have any idea of all the hardships that were to come in the next 2-1/2 years. All I felt at the moment was dread and loneliness.

We were assigned to support the 1st ROK Republic of Korea Division. We were so short of men at this time in the war that each man was assigned several jobs.

I was a BAR man (Browning Automatic Rifle), I drove a Jeep, and I was gunner on a 4.2 mortar. There were four ROKs (Republic of Korea soldiers) assigned to me as Squad leader because I could speak some Korean, having served before in Pusan at Camp Reese in 1948 with the 6th (Red Star) Division. I could not tell these four apart, so I called them "Fe, Fi, Fo, and Fum." They stayed with me all through combat.

At one point we were issued K Rations for three days. At about 2 A.M., one of my ROKs crawled into my tent so sick and let me know that all four of them were very sick. I got up and went to see what was wrong and what I could do for them.

I was astonished to find they had eaten all the rations for the three days at one time! They were very sick for several hours, but they all survived. However, at the time we thought they might not make it.

General MacArthur kept telling us to take 15 miles more, and

When the G.I.s were not fighting the weather, they were fighting the terrain. Korea is very mountainous. It was always up one mountain and down another. We had to take the same mountain again and again and again.

we did it again and again and again and again. We just kept on going. Seoul was taken approximately five times, but I wasn't there at the time. We took Serwan at least six times. Seoul wasn't secure when I arrived, and we were in the effort to take it the last time.

The Roadblock

Around the end of October 1950, we were at Onson north of P'yongyang with Company A 2nd Chemical Mortor Battallion, and we were assigned to hold the roadblock. The company was behind us. There were five Americans and fifteen ROKs at the roadblock. Suddenly I noticed a Korean woman walking down the road. We were on the lookout for suspicious vehicles but were not really watching for people. All at once for some reason the hair on the back of my neck stood up.

I left the others and approached the woman. She was dressed in black pants and top, and carried a radio on her back. Why someone had not already noticed the radio and become suspicious of what she was really doing there, I don't know. It turned out that she was radioing our position to her people. I immediately grabbed the receiver from her hand and put a gun to her head. I took her to the Command tent and turned her over to the C.O. who ordered the radio to be taken off her back.

I said, "Wait until I get out of here" because I was concerned that there might be a grenade under the radio. This was the only person I ever took captive. I was afraid we had the first suicide bomber in Korea, and I did not want to be the victim. I left the tent and went back to my job. I did not hear a grenade go off, so I guess she was clean, although I do not know what happened to her.

We immediately moved the roadblock for our safety because she had compromised our position. It did not do much good to move, however, because in a few hours we would be in enemy hands anyway.

We were attacked about 8 P.M., and we fought all night. The ammunition began to run low around midnight, and I went back to the company for some supplies. When I reached the company area, there was no one there and no ammunition to be had. I went back to the roadblock and told Ray Mendell and Arthur Welch, "They're all gone. I don't know where they are. Do you suppose they've taken up a new position?" None of us could figure out what had happened. Then we got a little busy as wave after wave of Chinese soldiers came at us.

In the morning an American plane came over and began to bomb and strafe the place where the company had been. We were concerned, but too busy to check on what was happening there. We later learned the company had left with only enough vehicles to move the wounded and their packs. Everything else was left behind—all the trucks, mortars, sleeping bags, and kitchen and hospital supplies. I thought about those supplies a lot as the days progressed, and we had nothing. (Of course we did not know any of these details until we returned home in 1953.)

We continued to fight, even though we were outnumbered. At daybreak we discovered what we were up against—the Chinese Communists had come across the Yalu River. We had previously heard rumors that the Chinese troops had crossed the Yalu River on October 28, 1950, when the Air Force had taken pictures of the build up. Our politicians, unfortunately, still did not believe the Chinese would become involved. We believed it when we looked up and saw what was coming at us. There they were— hordes of them—thousands and thousands of Chinese coming at us, screaming and yelling, and causing all the confusion they possibly could.

They came at us so quickly we could not shoot them fast enough. The BAR I was shooting was so hot that it began to fire automatically, and finally it just quit. When we ran out of ammunition, we began hand-to-hand combat. This went on for quite awhile, although I really can't tell how long, it seemed forever.

During the hand-to-hand combat I was stunned by a concussion grenade and knocked to the ground. A Chinese soldier pointed a Sub-Thompson machine gun in my face. The barrel looked like the opening of a 55-gallon drum; it was the biggest thing I had ever seen.

I put my right arm over my face, and I said, "LORD GOD, DON'T LET HIM SHOOT!" and the gun misfired.

He moved the gun to the man on my right, a Republic of Korea (ROK) soldier, and shot him. He moved the gun back to me while I continued to pray. The gun misfired again. He moved the gun to the man on my left, another ROK soldier, and killed him. Again he moved the gun back to me. He clicked the trigger again, and for the third time, the gun misfired. I will never know if it jammed, or if he was out of ammunition, but I believe the Lord was looking after me.

Frustrated at his attempts to kill me, the Chinese soldier gave me the worse beating I have ever had in my life before or since. But I was grateful to still be alive.

Finally, because their numbers were just too great, we were overrun. We did not surrender—we were captured about 9 A.M. November 2, 1950.

Chapter 2

A New Nightmare Begun

In that "moment in time," my life was changed forever. One part of the nightmare was over—the combat—and the other part—the captivity—had only just begun!

They took us five Americans captive and killed the fifteen ROKs on the spot. To the best of my recollection, I think this is when Fe, Fi, Fo, and Fum died. I was bleeding from my eyes, nose, mouth, and ears. I had a shrapnel wound in my ankle that I didn't even feel until later. I also had a bayonet wound inches from my spine.

At this point we were completely numb and confused. We could only follow orders, even if they were from our captors, especially if they were from our captors.

The Chinese tied our hands in front of us with Double E8 telephone wire and then ran it between our legs and tied it to the hands of the next man. That way we could not run.

We were taken to a ditch to wait for dark when we could move out. When we were put in the ditch, they had Lt. Deakin already tied up in there. We then found out what had happened. The company had pulled out some time in the night and left us. They had sent Lt. Deakin to tell us to withdraw, but he was captured on his way to us since we were already surrounded.

The names of the Americans captured that November morning were:

Lt. George Deakin
Raymond Mendell
Francis Spain
Arthur Welch
William "Bill" Smith

I am sorry to say the other four have passed away. Spain and Welch didn't come back from Korea, and Deakin and Mendell have passed away since our return. Mendell and I remained close friends during the dark days of our captivity as I shared earlier, and our families stayed close until his death.

We laid in the ditch all day long, dreading what would come next. Not knowing what that might be was the worst part. Fear and dread can make the mind do terrible things to you.

At dark the guards told us to get ready to leave, and we marched all night. At daylight we were put in a farm house so the American planes could not see us, and that evening we again proceeded north. We finally arrived at the Yuryong River where it was getting colder by the minute.

The guard ordered, "Take off all your clothes."

I crawled out on a rock and told Lt. Deakin, "I'm not going in that cold water. They can shoot me here. I would rather die dry than wet."

Lt. Deakin said, "Smith, look, they are taking off their clothes too, and you are a better man than they are." I reluctantly came off the rock and undressed as the others had done. We were ordered to put our clothes over our heads. We rolled our boots into our fatigues so we would not drop them, put the bundle over our heads, and started into the icy waters of the Kuryong River.

The guards knew just where to cross so the river would be only shoulder deep. It was not a swift current. If it had been, we might have lost some of the men in the dark. There were five prisoners and twelve to fifteen guards.

The water was not just cold—it was the coldest I have ever felt either before or since that day! It went right through my bones, and 55 years later I have still never felt entirely warm again. I expected to be shot at any time, especially when we came out of the water.

Suddenly the guard ordered, "Put your clothes on!"

I was never so surprised in my life. After we were dressed we continued to march north.

Hunger Pains

When I was captured, the Chinese and North Koreans took everything I had. If you had anything in your pockets, or wore a watch or rings, they took it. But for some reason they overlooked a small tube of toothpaste that I had in my breast pocket. I do not know why they missed this, but they did; and I would always be grateful for that.

My friend Ray Mendell and I ate the toothpaste for the first eight days of our captivity. When the tube was empty, we turned it inside out and licked it clean. I took the button off my field jacket and put it in my mouth to make saliva. The button was green when I started to suck it, and it was white before I finished with it. (Always remember if you are in a position of being without water, take the button from your clothes and put it in your mouth to make saliva. It is not wonderful, but it will help.)

The toothpaste was the only food I had for the first eight days, and I had no drinking water except for the snow I was able to melt. At the end of that time, we were given a bowl of frozen sorghum. I chewed on it and let it melt in my mouth. It had no taste, but at least it helped fill my stomach.

The hunger pains were so awful, and they were only just beginning. Now when I hear someone say they are hungry, I just smile. They don't know what real hunger feels like.

The hunger that would be our constant companion was the most gut-wrenching, mind-numbing, physically debilitating feeling that any human could experience. It didn't last for a day or two—it lasted the entire time of our captivity. In my case it was 2-1/2 years. It was no wonder we could not eat at first when we returned home. Our bodies had been in a starvation mode for so long that it took a while to convince them they were FREE and could eat all they wanted.

I still go to the grocery store, stand in the aisles, look at the vast array of food, and marvel at the options we have. Any person who has had his freedom taken away as a POW and has felt the cruelty of an enemy who hates you, just has a different outlook on the world. I hope no one has to ever again feel the hunger I felt in the prison camp.

I ate everything I could get my hands on in the 2-1/2 years of my captivity. I started off with the toothpaste, next I ate the cracked corn and millet they gave us, and then over time I had sorghum, seaweed, magpie, pig weed, sometimes vegetables, and sometimes food infested with maggots. We ate anything we could get, especially the first winter. It was only after the peace talks began that the food improved a little.

When I say we ate vegetables, it was usually a cabbage we could steal and throw in a pot of boiling water. It gave the water a little flavor, but not enough to give us any strength. That is why I lost 113 pounds during the 2-1/2 years of captivity. The food was so meager, I don't know how any of us survived.

When we made soup with seaweed and ate it, it came out just like it went in. I know that is not a pretty fact, but nevertheless it is true. When we were given food with maggots in it—usually fish—we were so hungry that we ate it anyway and worried about what the maggots would do to us later. At that point, we really didn't care because we were so hungry.

At times some of the guys were so sick and lethargic, they just gave up and would not eat. We had to make them become so mad at us that they would eat out of spite. I did not care why they were eating, I only cared that we could get them to swallow something. I have force fed several of my buddies, and this technique was used on me in the Valley in 1950-51 when I was sick and would not eat. Tomlinson and his helpers put the food in my mouth and held it shut until I swallowed. If they had not done that, I would surely have died. So you can see we had to help each other to stay alive.

When I came home and married, I told my wife to always put enough on my table to eat because I might go naked and be cold again, but I would never be hungry again. The lack of food for so long created unusual habits in us after we returned. For a long time, I had a habit of hiding food in the drawers in our bedroom. It had become second nature to me to try to protect myself during captivity, and it took a long time to overcome that habit. I also always carried a snack in my pocket when we went out for a drive on Sunday afternoons. It is unbelievable what you will do to try and protect yourself even when the danger is past. You do these things subconsciously. After we returned home, I knew I could have food or a snack anytime, but I still felt better if I knew where some food was at all times.

14

For a long time it was also difficult for me if my wife threw out anything from the table. She learned to just put the leftovers in the refrigerator and clean it out when I wasn't around. I didn't know that until later. As I said, POW wives learn ways to live with the results of our experiences and how to make our lives a lot easier for us.

The March

Our captors collected prisoners for several days. After we were captured we were put into school houses, caves, mud huts, farm houses, tunnels, or any kind of shelter they could find to keep us out of sight of the U.S. planes. We were hidden during the day and did all our marching at night. This made it much more difficult, but it was the only way to keep us out of sight.

They did not want our planes to see us because they did not want our troops to mount a rescue effort. It certainly was not for our comfort that we were put into any shelter. They were not concerned about where we were kept.

I lost track of time, but Ray and I decided we must have marched about 30 days. We started the march with about 750 men, and when we arrived at a semi-permanent camp, we only had 250 men. This was a huge loss of men for only 30 days of marching.

I don't think we marched straight north; I think we zigzagged back and forth across Korea, so there is no way to tell how far the march could have been. I only know it was a very long, very tiring, very cold, and very, very hungry and thirsty time for all of us.

As the march progressed we carried the wounded because we saw what would happen to them if we left them behind. If they could not walk and had no one to help them or if they fell behind, we heard gunshots and knew they had been killed. So we made makeshift litters and carried anyone who needed it, even though most of us were wounded too. Unbelievably, some of the men refused to help with the wounded, and to this day I don't see how they can look at themselves in the mirror. Usually the ones who refused to help were officers. I lost all respect for most of them on that march.

One night in particular stands out in my mind. We had been carrying an ROK soldier for several hours. We stopped to rest, and I leaned down to ask him if he was all right. He became frightened, jumped up from the litter, and ran. I yelled. Someone down the line grabbed him and broke his neck.

After we reached Camp 5, we learned that some of the other men who were captured were taken to Korean villages and marched through the village naked. They were ridiculed and spat upon. At least I didn't have that humiliation.

The nights all seemed to blur together. I don't know how long we had been marching when we found ourselves between two tunnels. Suddenly the mountain began to roar and tremble. At first we didn't know what was happening, but then the side of the mountain started sliding down on us.

There were some men in the path of the slide who didn't have a chance. The earth came sliding so fast nobody could do anything. There was no time nor place to run. The men were swept down the mountain and buried by the rubble. We never knew how many died there, but we always thought there were quite a few. The slide happened about 100 feet ahead of where I was walking. We had to quickly climb over the rocks and dirt to continue to keep up with the column of our men.

For once I was in the right place at the right time, and I survived the slide. A few more minutes and I would have been in the middle of it. Again, the Lord was with me, as He was all the time, but especially that moment of time in Korea.

Chapter 3

The March Continued

About two weeks after we were captured, we were in a mud hut where we had been put for the day to rest, again out of sight of our planes. The planes seemed to be coming over very frequently. I think they were searching for our position. They were so close and still so far away.

The Chinese called all of us out of the hut. The interrogator then brought a lieutenant out and stood him at attention in front of the group.

The interrogator said, "How many men are over that hill?" Well, the lieutenant gave his name, rank, and serial number, as required by the Geneva Convention and the American Government.

At this, the interrogator became angry. The question was repeated, and the answer was repeated. This happened a third time. By then I thought the interrogator was going to have a stroke. He stopped for a minute in front of the lieutenant. Then he took out his small pistol and blew the lieutenant's brains out. We were all so shocked that we just stood very still while the guards dragged the lieutenant's body away.

The interrogator went back into the hut and came out with a sergeant. They stood him in front of the group and said to him, "How many men are over that hill?"

He answered, "A whole damn regiment!" Of course he did not know anything about the movement of troops, but it satisfied the interrogator, and he walked off.

Now you tell me who was the smarter soldier—the lieutenant who could never fight again, or the sergeant who would live to fight another day? Thankfully, after Korea, Congress changed the Articles of War so that a captured soldier can reveal more than just name, rank, and serial number. It gives them authority to share, "what it takes to survive that does not betray your fellow man or this country."

I think one thing I am resentful of was the fact that we were captured in summer uniforms because our winter clothes had not been shipped to us yet. They were still on the dock in San Diego because the Longshoremen's Union was on strike for higher wages and would not load the ships.

Those longshoremen slept at home in good, warm, clean beds, with no lice, plenty of water, a shower every day, no hunger pains, no cold, no freezing rain or snow, and wore nice, warm clothes. They did not care about Bill Smith or Ray Mendell or Vince Simonetti or Joe Whoever you were. They only wanted more money.

We finally received a blanket from the Communists in late winter 1950. It still didn't come from the longshoremen in the form of a uniform. The first uniform I had came from the Communists in the summer of 1951. I was even more resentful because it came from them, but by this time our uniforms were in tatters and rags, and we were forced to accept whatever they gave us.

Here we were all these miles from home, fighting for our freedom and theirs for $1.50 a day plus meals (when we could get them), and we were freezing to death. In fact some of the guys did freeze to death while the longshoremen were striking for higher wages. I still become angry about this when I let myself think about it or when my feet and hands begin to ache because they were frozen, and I know those clothes could have helped us so much.

Unforgettable People

Lt. William Funchess came into my life about this time. He was from another outfit, but that didn't matter when a man was wounded and needed help. He was shot in the ankle and could walk only a little. We could not leave him behind so Mendell, Welch, and I took turns carrying him on our backs. I carried him across a river, and I remember his foot dragging in the water. The pain was so bad, he couldn't keep from crying out. I also remember carrying him over a one-man bridge. The three of us thought he was worth the effort.

After we reached Pyoktong, the guards made us leave him. It was the hardest thing we ever did because we were afraid of what would happen to him. I laid him on the ground of a schoolhouse in the dark. I leaned over and said, "Hang in there, someone else will take care of you from here on." I really didn't think that would happen, but I was trying to keep his spirits up. I thought, *He is as good as dead.* I felt bad about lying to him and to myself, but I had no other choice.

Later I searched for him through all the camps I was in, but I never ran into him in Korea. I continued to search when I returned to the states. I didn't know if he had returned or not, but I never forgot him.

In 1999 my wife was working the registration desk at the

Korean EX-POW Convention in Macon, Georgia, when Lt. Funchess and his wife walked up to register. My wife was thrilled to see them because she knew how much I wanted to find him. She asked him to stay right there and quickly went to find me. No one can imagine the shock of us seeing each other again after all those years. Neither of us knew if the other had survived, and finally we were together again.

There are so many of the guys who are closer to me than my own brother that it would be impossible to mention them all—the guys from the march, Camp 5, and especially Camp 2 Company 3. I could go on and on, but you know who you are.

One memorable character entered my life during that march in North Korea in 1950 and has woven in and out of my life for the last 56 years. Bob Cavaganaro is a wonderful friend. I mention him in particular because we met in such an odd way.

In the winter of 1950, I finally was able to get a hold of some water in a helmet. I think two guys had already used the water before I finally had a chance. It was really dirty, but it felt so good on my feet that I didn't care. I saw a kid watching me. You had to be careful because one man watching you could be the lookout for a group of men who intended to jump you and take your water. This kid kept watching me very closely.

Finally, after five to ten minutes, he finally got up the courage to ask, "Could I have that water when you are done?"

He was alone. He had on a pair of glasses he had taken from a dead soldier. They were broken, and he had wired them together. They were better than nothing, but just barely.

I looked up at him and said, "Get your own damn water." It frightened him enough so that he left me alone, which is what I had wanted him to do. Despite our first encounter, we eventually became good friends in Camp 2 Company 3, the reactionary camp, in the summer of 1952.

This story shows how small the world really is. My brother-in-law, Gene, worked for the *Washington Post* newspaper in 1975 with a guy named Bob Cavaganaro. One day the conversation was about the war, and Bob said, "I was a POW in Korea." Gene said, "So was my brother-in-law, Bill Smith." Cavaganaro said, "I knew a Smith over there. I think his name was Bill. Maybe he is the same one."

Gene gave him my phone number, and Bob called me that very night. Sure enough, we were the ones who had known each other in Korea. We talked several times and were so glad to find each other after 22 years.

Five years later, my wife and I were on vacation at Myrtle Beach, South Carolina, and someone knocked on the door of our motel room. I looked at my wife and said, "No one knows we are here except Lisa" (our daughter). So we were quite surprised by the knock.

I answered the door, and there stood a tall guy with his glasses sitting crookedly on his face. I didn't recognize him until he said, "Get your own damn water." I knew instantly it was Cavaganaro. We talked for a long time. He was vacationing at the beach too, and when he found out we were there, he decided to look us up.

We had to learn early in our captivity at Pyoktong who you could and could not trust. Your very life depended on your being right. I quickly knew I could trust Cavaganaro. He did everything he could to harass the Communists just like some of the rest of us were doing. He was very much against the lectures and the brain-washing techniques.

That is why in the summer of 1952 we both ended up in Camp 2 Company 3 with the 115 UN prisoners the Chinese had labeled Reactionaries. The Chinese said there was no hope for us, and that was fine with us. We would do the work and not give them any more trouble if they would stop the lectures. And that is exactly what happened.

Seeing Cavaganaro at Myrtle Beach was just like being back in Korea in 1952. It was as if the 27 years had not passed at all. Now we see Bob at the Korean POW Convention every year, and we are good friends with him and his wife, Lilianne.

Dangerous Pests

The lice started to bother us on the march, and they became really bad when we reached The Valley in the winter of 1950. There were so many of them. One of the doctors, who had been captured at the same time, told us we had to try to keep them off us because in our weakened condition, they could drink all the blood from our bodies in only 36 hours.

When we heard this we tore our clothes off and turned them inside out. We burned a stick until it was red hot, cooled it a little, and ran it down the seams of our clothes to kill the eggs. It was a never-ending battle, and this procedure had to be done every day by every single man. If anyone in the hut did not do the same thing, it was a lost cause. Still the lice were so bad. Of course, another reason they were so bad was because we didn't have any water, and the sanitation wasn't the best in the world.

To this day if I see a man with a full beard or very long hair, I can feel the lice crawling on my face, and I automatically begin to scratch my face and scalp.

Devastation Along the Way

At one point on the long march, we stayed at what we called the Mining Camp—at the site of an abandoned coal mine. As we moved from camp to camp, we named them ourselves, and you would be surprised how the names quickly spread among the troops. We all knew exactly what the other one was talking about.

I can't remember how long we stayed at the Mining Camp, but once again we were kept hidden so our planes could not see us.

The guys started to die in large numbers there because they could not eat. We mixed the cracked corn and millet with water and cooked it, but it was still very difficult to eat. Our bodies had not yet adjusted to it or the harsh living conditions. It was the first time we were all together in such a large number. We were with the approximately 250 men who had survived the death march out of the original 750 with which we had begun.

After the Mining Camp, we moved to the Bean Camp. In my mind I remember this camp as part of the Upper Valley. As I said, we were kept dazed, confused, and off balance all the time so some of the exact details remain hazy to us. Afterwards, we moved into the Lower Valley for a period of what seemed like two weeks. The conditions were about the same there—a mud hut to live in, no heat, the same food (and very little of it), and the same cold to endure. The only thing that distinguished this camp from the others on the march is the fact that we spent our first Christmas in captivity here, and I will never forget that Christmas dinner.

The Dog

Ray Mendell and I had the good fortune to be in the right place at the right time again. A small dog about the size of a large coon had the misfortune to be in the wrong place at the wrong time. Anyway, he ended up being the Christmas dinner for a lot of very hungry G.I.s. We had not had very much to eat since the beginning of November, and the little dog was certainly a Christmas present sent from God. We killed him, put him in a pot, and made soup out of him. I don't know how many people ate the soup that cold December day; I only know nothing ever tasted so good.

I know it may sound repulsive to some people to eat a dog, but when you are as hungry as we were, you will eat just about anything. The only thing I actually remember turning down was a worm-infested horse, but that is another story you will hear about later.

Humans have a strong desire to stay alive and therefore in times of privation, the body takes over. You eat whatever you can get and don't think much about what it is. As I think about it now, I wonder how I could have done it, but at the time, I never gave it a thought. I only enjoyed what God had provided for me.

In 1998, I was standing in the lobby of the Radisson Hotel in Norfolk, Virginia, talking to some of my buddies at a Korean EX-POW Convention. Someone walked up to me and said, "Eat any good dog lately?" My world stopped. For a minute I was in the kitchen in The Valley in Korea on that cold Christmas Day in 1950. I didn't remember his face because there had been so many of us and we were so hungry, but I remembered, "THE DOG." He put his arms around me and said, "I never tasted soup as good as that soup was."

We held on to each other for a long time. My wife had heard the story, but the reality was a shock. It was a shock for his wife too. We talked and talked and later went out to dinner with our wives. My wife loves this couple. They are Sylvia and Robert Hibdon, but she calls them Sylvia and "Dog." He just laughs because it is with love and affection she does it. That name will always be his. They live in Tennessee, and we really look forward to seeing them at the EX-POW Convention. We talk on the phone two or three times in between, and we are so glad to know they are all right, as all right as a POW can be, that is.

The Hard Winter

We arrived in Pyoktong from The Valley, a very weary, rag tag bunch of young men. We were there for one day when our planes came over and began to drop bombs. They did not know that American POWs were present in the area when the bombing started. Some of the wounded got off the litters and ran up the side of the mountain faster than the ones who had carried them. I just stood there. I figured I might run into a bomb, so I may as well stand still. If it was going to get me, it was going to get me, so

The captured troops in Korea were subjected to such bad weather—40-60 degrees below zero along with much snow. When we were captured, we had on sumer uniforms and quickly began to freeze. Some G.I.s actually froze to death because of the clothing.

why run? We stayed in that area until dark and then started the long 20-mile march back to The Valley. Now we really were worn out.

It went down to 40 to 60 degrees below zero, and we were freezing to death. We would step outside of the hut to urinate, and it would freeze before it hit the ground. There was a stack of urine three to four feet high. It was the darndest thing I ever saw.

The effects of starvation, beri-beri, diarrhea, pneumonia, parasites, and lice caused so many deaths during the winter of 1950-51 that it was almost impossible to bury the bodies fast enough. We stacked them up like cord wood.

The look of the men was scary. Everyone was down to 100-110 pounds, and that is terrible for men who are six feet tall. Our eyes were sunk about an inch back in their sockets. We all looked like scarecrows with our sunken eyes, long beards, skinny arms, and toothpick legs. We would find out years later just how hard these conditions were on our bodies.

When we returned home we were told it would be hard, if not impossible, to father children because of the effects of the malnutrition in our early years. I am happy to say that this turned out to be untrue, and I have a beautiful daughter. We were also told that our major organs would be 20 years older than our chronological age. They said the effects of our captivity would really begin to take its toll on us after the age of 35, and unfortunately, they were right on that account. I had my first heart attack at the age of 43.

It is unbelievable what the human body can withstand. Nature moves in and takes over for you when you have no choice and you can't help yourself. The food we were given was enough to keep us alive, but only barely. I expect that was part of the plan. They were able to brainwash us all day, every day, and try to turn some of the weaker ones to their way of thinking.

There was not enough food for us to be strong enough to make much trouble for them and certainly not enough energy to successfully escape. Several of us tried, but to the best of my recollection, I do not know of anyone who made a successful escape from captivity in Korea. There may have been some, but I do not know about them.

At this time, our food consisted of cracked corn and millet. At first we received one small bowl a day and one small bowl of water. Later, we received two bowls a day unless we were on hard labor and then back to one each. While we were in The Valley, they began to add a few soybeans. In late 1951 in Camp 5 they added sorghum periodically. This was barely enough to keep us alive. When we returned home we had to very slowly eat six to eight times a day until our systems became accustomed to food again.

In The Valley in the winter of 1950-1951, we were so cold and so hungry there is no way I can tell you vividly enough how bad it really was. Sometimes a guard would come to the door of the hut and throw a handful of soybeans on the floor just to see the men fight for them. Then he would stand back and laugh and watch the fight. I decided that I would die of hunger before I gave him the satisfaction of moving after a bean when he threw them. I tried to talk the others into not going after the beans, but they were so hungry, they didn't care. Finally, he tired of the game and stopped it altogether.

Later in 1951 we would make bean curd. It didn't have any taste to me but it was something to help the hunger pains. After we cooked the cracked corn and millet or whatever we had, we took the crust from the sides and bottom of the pot and boiled them with water until they turned black. HOORAY, HOORAY, COFFEE!

Attempt to Escape

My friend Harry Gennaro and I decided to try an escape before we became any more malnourished and weak, and before we were any further away from our lines. We decided if we headed south, we would run into our lines.

In preparation, we stole corn and soybeans, and parched them. We had enough for about three days if we were careful, so we were ready. We left right after roll call and just before daybreak and headed south. We had gone about seven to ten miles when we ended up in the middle of a communications center. We had been free for two days.

We were captured by the home guard (young boys with wooden guns training to be soldiers) and turned over to the soldiers. We told the soldiers, "We were on a wood detail and got lost." There was a wood detail every day so we had the story ready, just in case we were caught. They seemed to believe us.

They asked, "Where is your wood?" I said, "It was heavy and we threw it away." We really felt like we were going to get away with it, and the wood detail story would be fine. We knew they could shoot us for the escape attempt if they wanted. We had just started to relax when the Chinese sergeant in charge of the wood detail every day was brought into the room. He said, "We didn't have a wood detail today."

Gennaro and I knew we were in for it then. The beating immediately started. After the initial beating was over, they started marching us back to the main camp. They beat and kicked and hit us with rifle butts and spat on us every step of the way back to The Valley. That was a very long seven miles.

When we reached The Valley, they put us in a corn crib for several days as part of our punishment. There was corn on the floor, and we were eating pretty well and sleeping fairly warm in the corn shucks. When the guards figured out it didn't seem to be bothering us, they pulled us out of the corn crib and sent us back to the general population. This was my first attempt at escape; it would not be the last.

We had wood detail every day, which is why Gennaro and I felt safe using this as an excuse for our escape from The Valley in 1950. We were always sent into the woods to find wood to cook with and to burn so we would not freeze. We also stole any source of wood we could find in camp.

All the fences were stripped, as well as the shingles from the roof of the huts. Everything that could burn would suddenly disappear. Camp 5 was completely stripped of wood during the winter of 1950. I was caught stealing shingles from the Chinese guard house, and I was punished very severely. It made the guards angry since that was their quarters. Everyone who was caught stealing wood was punished. The punishments for this offense could be anything that the guard decided he wanted it to be and last as long as they wanted the punishments to last, from a few minutes, to a few hours, to a few months.

The Lord's Prayer

Prayer was an important part of my getting through my captivity. There were some days during my captivity when I was not conscious and could not pray, but every day that I could, I always prayed the Lord's Prayer. I always thought that one wonderful prayer covered everything, and I still say it every day. It gave me the strength to carry on in Korea, and it fortifies me every day now. Of course, I tried to pray more than just that simple prayer, but many times I was not able to do it. That prayer was my mainstay throughout the entire captivity.

I thank God every day for what I have, and believe me, I really know what I have. When you are reduced to nothing for a time and then return to the bounty that we have here in our country, you are truly grateful. I hope I never forget to thank the Lord every day.

Chapter 4

Camp Life

During the winter of 1950-1951 we lost 1600-2200 men. We could not keep count. That was the worse time of my captivity. What caused all these deaths? I think there were three main things that by and large were responsible for so much loss of life:

First: Initially after our capture, we were dazed and confused. This is the way the enemy wanted us to be so they tried to keep us that way. Anything they could do to keep us in a state of perpetual, emotional turmoil seemed good to them. They did not want us to get back on our feet and begin to think like soldiers. That would have been bad for them because then we could have organized and taken care of ourselves. They also did not want to have their authority questioned.

Second: The food, what there was of it, was impossible to eat. Each day there were usually two small bowls of cracked corn and millet cooked with boiling water (like oatmeal) and two bowls of water. If you were being punished, however, there was only one bowl of each.

Third: The cold weather, the worst in Korean history that year, along with the summer uniforms we wore, only added to our misery. There were parasites, diarrhea, untreated wounds, pneumonia, and by this time most of us were beginning to feel the effects of malnutrition. By the end of the winter, most of the men were down to about 100 pounds. These were all contributing factors to the high loss of life that winter.

Permanent Camp

After we left the Lower Valley in January 1951, we returned to Pyoktong to set up Camp 5 to become our permanent camp in North Korea. Pyoktong was a Korean village on the Yalu River. The village was on a peninsula, and the Chinese simply moved all the people out, put a fence across the opening, and they had a camp. It was an easy way for them to make a permanent home for nearly 3000 men who would eventually come to Camp 5. There were about 1200 men in the camp at most times, according to most reports I have read. There were approximately 300 huts in the compound.

Most of the U.N. prisoners would at one time or another pass through Camp 5. It was the largest POW camp in Korea. The camp was divided into several parts: Uptown, Downtown, and The Temple

Camp 5

ESTABLISHED: January 1951-August 1953

LOCATION: The west end of the town of Pyoktong. Koreans were removed from the west end of the town and the POWs were housed in the empty huts. This was the first permanent POW camp.

This is a picture of Camp 5 in North Korea. The village of Pyaktong was taken over in order to construct it. The Chinese put a fence across the peninsula, moved out the natives, and took over the huts to get an instant POW camp.

The land was surrounded by the waters of the Yahu River and on two sides by China. If you stood on the very end point of land, you faced China and on the right was the hillside where we buried so many of our friends. This was one of the largest camps in Korea. At one time or another, nearly every prisoner passed through Camp 5.

PRISON POPULATION: When the camp first opened, there were a large number of POWs, but the death rate was high and the number of prisoners decreased continually. Typically it held about 1200 men.

SECURITY: The camp was separated from the town by a four or five foot barbed wire fence, which dissected the peninsula. The camp underwent many reorganizations, but the security remained fairly simple. Approximately 200 Chinese manned 10 to 12 posts in the camp, and an estimated 1200 to 1500 additional Chinese soldiers were located in the village of Pyoktong. The soldiers were not directly involved with the security of the camp but could be called if needed.

CONDITIONS: This camp was known for an intense Chinese indoctrination program effort. Most POWs resisted the indoctrination and were often tortured and beaten. Food was inadequate, consisting of cracked corn and millet. The prisoners had severe weight loss. The medical treatment was primitive.

Shortly after our arrival at Camp 5, I was called to headquarters with another man. I have tried to remember who he was, but I can't remember his name.

I was told, "W.W. Smith, You will be the monitor." The other man was to be the squad leader. Neither of us knew what the Chinese expected of us. About a week later we were taken back to headquarters, and I found out what they wanted. They wanted me to squeal on the other men.

They set me in a chair. The interrogator said, "W.W. Smith, what did the men say in the hut during the day, and what did they say at night?" I knew I was not going to tell him anything, so I said, "They don't talk." This made him very angry. He repeated the question. I repeated the answer. After this went on for a few minutes, he became more angry, looked at me, and said, "You are not a good monitor. You will be the squad leader." The other man was made the monitor, and that suited me just fine because I knew I would never do or say anything that would hurt a POW. I would later pay dearly for that decision, but I never regretted making it.

Our lives were completely unpredictable. One of the hardest parts of the whole ordeal was the complete lack of control over anything in your life. It is hard to explain the feelings you have when you are under the pressure that we were under and the enemy has complete control over you. I finally came to realize I could do nothing. They had control over when I awoke or slept, ate or didn't eat, stayed indoors or came out. They even had control over whether I took my next breath or not.

Giving the Situation to God

The only thing I could keep from them was my mind, and I gave myself and the situation to God. We all wanted to live, but we considered ourselves as dead men. Whenever I gave control of the situation to God, I was at ease in my mind and they could not defeat me. I was always able to endure the torture, the brainwashing, and everything they could do to me and survive.

It was the most difficult thing in the world to keep my mind busy, but I felt I had won when the enemy could not touch my mind. They really did horrible things to my body, and it was the worst 2-1/2 years of my life, but they did not win because they never reached my mind.

Camp 5 is the camp where I was in the most trouble with the Chinese. I could not sit idly by and let all the propaganda and terrible things they said about my country go unanswered. Every time I stood up for myself or my country, I took the consequences. Sometimes the consequences were almost more than a human body could live through. Sometimes the consequences could cause unconsciousness. Sometimes the consequences could cause starvation. Although I was already starving, they made it worse. Sometimes the consequences could last for hours, or weeks, or even months. And always you wondered if you would live through them. I only know I did survive only by the grace of God.

In that horrible cold winter of 1950-1951 in North Korea, the lectures began early and lasted late. We were made to sit or squat on the frozen ground in our summer uniforms for eight to ten hours a day. You can only imagine how cold we felt. Even if we had wanted to listen to the lecture, we were too cold to try.

Communism Versus Democracy

Over and over again, we were told we were "cannon fodder for the Wall Street warmongers." We were 18-, 19- and 20-year-olds. We didn't know anything about Wall Street, nor did we care, so that argument fell on dead ears.

We were also told their way of life was better than ours. I really don't know how they could expect us to think we were better off in the situation in Korea with no food, no heat, no medical treatment, nor anything that added to our creature comfort, than we were in the U.S. where we had an abundance of everything. They tried to convince us that their way of life would be better for the world than democracy.

If Communism is so good, why are so many people still starving to death under this form of government in North Korea today while the people of South Korea are prospering under democracy? We did our best to prevent the spread of this menace in 1950, and I am sorry we could not have liberated the entire North so the people would be free of this scourge today. Well, I had lived under both forms of government, and I could see ours had theirs beat all to hell and back as far as I was concerned.

In the summer of 1951 we were finally given new uniforms, Chinese style. They were blue drawstring pants, thin blue jackets, blue bill caps, and tennis shoes. The new uniforms helped with the lice a little bit. It did not get rid of the problem completely, but it helped. Our old clothes were taken away, along with our boots. Some of the guys hid their boots until they could take the shanks out of them to make knives. It was the last time we would ever see our boots.

One reason our uniforms were taken was not to help us but for propaganda's sake. Some of the guys were made to put on the best of the Chinese uniforms and parade for the cameras. After the pictures were taken, those special uniforms were taken away again. Thank the good Lord I was not chosen to be in the parade. If you were told to do it, there was nothing you could do but comply with the command.

More new uniforms were issued to us before the really bad weather of the winter of 1951-1952. These uniforms were blue and heavily padded. They were very warm, thank goodness, but we still had tennis shoes.

We were still made to sit outdoors and listen to the lectures for eight to ten hours at a time when it was 50 to 60 below zero, but this year the uniforms made the bitter cold a little easier to bear than the winter before. The lectures, however, were still the same.

About a year after my capture, the Chinese turned on loud speakers, and the lectures went on day and night for about sixteen to twenty hours a day. I don't know how long this continued because, thankfully, I was transferred out.

It was easy to give a logical rebuttal to most of the pro-Communist arguments they gave us. That is what made them so mad with the 115 reactionaries who would eventually be sent to Camp 2 Company 3. We always had an answer and were not afraid to express it. That is why I was transferred out in the summer of 1952. That was the last time I ever saw Camp 5, and I can't say I was sorry.

Friends for Life

One day a water faucet was put in the compound, and afterwards there were a lot of fights because people didn't want to stand in line for their turn. The guard didn't interfere; he just stood there and watched. I was in line one day with a lot of Americans when a big Brit came up and tried to jump the line. An American denied him access, so the fight was on. It lasted for about two hours. The guard let the fight continue as long as it didn't get out of control. I stepped up to watch the American's back and see that no one else jumped in the fray, so it was a fair fight. We later learned that the Brit was a Regimental Boxing Champ, but the American G.I. sure gave him a good beating. The American's name was Joe Ascue, and he became one of the best buddies I had in captivity. From that day on, we watched each other's backs and probably saved each other's life on several occasions. The Joe that I speak of in the rest of the book will be this great friend.

I am proud to have been friends with so many good and faithful men, and I am happy to be able to look them in the face and call them friend. I know I did nothing to harm any one of them while I was in captivity. There were a few who made life miserable for the rest of us, but they have to live with themselves and look in the mirror every day. I would not change places with them for anything in the world.

I believe if Joe and I had not gone through the things we did and ended up in that terrible place in Korea, my life would have taken a very different turn. I do not know what it would have been like, but it would have been different.

I certainly never would have gone to Bluefield, West Virginia, and therefore I never would have met Charlotte. I look back and wonder where I would have ended up because my life was in such turmoil when I arrived at Bluefield. I am sure God was again directing my path and again working in mysterious ways to protect me. It did not seem so at the time, but God was setting me up for the next 50 years when Joe and I met in that hell hole that was Korea.

Chapter 5

Punishments

I believe one of the reasons I had it so hard and always stayed in trouble with the guards was because I was with the 2nd Chemical Mortor Battallion. The North Koreans and the Chinese immediately thought we were carrying on chemical or germ warfare because the equipment we were captured with had the company emblem with the word "chemical" on it. Once they had their minds made up about something, there was no changing them, so I just suffered the consequences. (Of course we were not engaged in chemical warfare, but I could never convince them that the American government did not use chemicals or germs in battle.) So my punishments came a little swifter and a little harder than some of the others.

There were various punishments we had to endure at the camps. When I speak of being taken to headquarters for interrogation, a "chat," for an "interview," or use any of the words the guards used to call a "visit," in this chapter you will see what could and did happen to me.

The following punishments all were given to me at one time or another; either individually or in groups at one time. Now do not misunderstand, I was not the only one that this ever happened to and I do not claim to be. I am simply one of the fortunate ones who, by the grace of God, was able to survive them.

Believe me I know a lot of good and courageous men who did not survive these punishments, and over the years I have often wondered, "Why did I?" I never signed a confession at any time while I was a POW because I did not do anything that I felt I needed to confess. Sometimes I took the consequences for this decision, but I was never sorry I made it.

Most of the time you didn't know what the offense was that you were being punished for, and some of the time there was no offense at all, so I will just give you a brief description of the Chinese forms of punishments rather than try to remember when or why they happened to me during my captivity.

The Hole

"The Hole" was just that—a hole in the ground. It was only big enough to get into. You sat in it with your knees practically under your chin. You could not straighten your legs out or even turn right or left; you could only sit.

There was a piece of steel put over the opening of the hole, just above your head. When it got very cold in winter, you nearly froze, and in the summer, the sun beat down on the steel and nearly cooked your head.

You never knew how long you would be left in The Hole. The Chinese put you there at their own whim, for however long they decided—anywhere from several hours to several weeks. While you were there, you were forced to sit in your own excrement.

The Hole was approximately 75 yards from the compound. I

was put in there several times. When I was in it, my buddy Joe Ascue would steal food, crawl out, and drop it in to me. When Joe was in The Hole, I would feed him the same way because the guards would not feed you when you were there.

If either one of us had been caught giving food to the other, we would have been shot. But if we had not done this for each other, we both would probably have died. This is what I mean by a friend you could count on to watch your back. It was necessary to have at least one buddy like this in order to survive. I was very fortunate that I had several friends like Joe, and most of us came back alive, partly because we relied on each other.

Frost Bite

My feet and hands could have frozen any time during the march because they were so cold and wet all the time, but I don't think they did. I was very fortunate. When I finally did experience it during one of the other tortures, I met a Philippine lieutenant, who came into The Temple when I was working there on hard labor, and he told me what to do. I do not know if he was a doctor or not, but he seemed to know a little about medicine. He said he didn't have anything to give me for frost bite, but if I would wiggle my fingers and toes as much as possible and keep them as dry as possible, I might be able to save them. I did as he told me, and I didn't lose any part of my fingers or toes like some of the guys did.

I still suffer from the frost bite even after 55 years—the cold weather hurts me so bad even though I always wear heavy socks, gloves, and boots when I go out in the cold. I stay in as much as possible in the winter. I think the worse part is the fact that my feet sweat all the time and stay cold all the time. The doctor told me to wear white socks and tennis shoes wide enough to accommodate my feet—in my case 6E. When I am in the house, they recommend sheep's wool lined bedroom slippers because the wool will absorb the moisture, and my feet will stay warmer.

I do not know what happened to the Philippine lieutenant. I never saw him again but I certainly owe him a great deal. I am very grateful for what he did for me in Korea.

The Chinese Water Treatment

In this form of punishment, you were tied spread-eagled to a table. A very small hole was punctured in a bucket of water, and a string was inserted in the bucket. Then the bucket was hung over your head approximately six to eight inches above your face and between your eyes.

The water dripped down on your forehead and continued until you thought you would lose your mind. Some of the men nearly did go crazy. I was very fortunate. When I had that punishment, I was able to endure it.

Sleep Deprivation

During this torture, the instructor kept you awake as long as he wanted. The length of time depended on the individual instructor and how mad he was at the time. He asked you the same questions over and over again. There was no way you could answer them because you were just an enlisted man. You didn't know the answers, but the questions never stopped.

Sometimes you were kept awake 24 to 36 hours, making you become numb. I know maybe that doesn't sound like a long time, but most of the time you were made to stand up at attention. Some of the time they would let you sit down, but only for a short while. You never got to lay down at all, and you were never left alone for a moment. The voices would come and go. They hammered at you relentlessly.

The Rafters

The Chinese would take you to the guard house and ask questions. If they didn't get the answers they wanted, they would tie your wrists to the rafters and pull you up so your feet would not touch the floor. Sometimes you were not very far off the floor, maybe just inches. They just made sure your feet did not touch. You would hang there for as long as it pleased the Chinese. Again, it all depended on the instructor, the mood he was in, how mad he was, and how the war was going for their side—almost anything could influence how long they would torture you this way.

Your shoulders would sometimes come out of their sockets. Your hands would always get numb. You would never know how long this would go on. The psychological torture was, if possible, worse than the physical. After a while the pain became so bad you would pass out, but you could not shut your mind off as easily.

Russian Roulette

I think this was one of the worse punishments we had to endure. The guards would sit you on a chair, put a gun to your head, and pull the trigger. If you were lucky the gun just snapped, but you never knew if this would happen or not. The bullet could be in its chamber one second and just as easily in your brain the next.

If the trigger clicked, you drew another deep breath and thanked God, but it was not over that quickly. They moved around you, put the gun to the back of your head, and tried again. You held your breath, and the gun clicked again. You breathed once more, and you thanked God again.

The next time could be the last, and the bullet could slam into your brain at any minute. This was part of the psychological torture of it. This could go on for a long time until you realize the gun may not be loaded at all. They could have changed guns at anytime while they were behind you, so this torture really worked on your mind.

To this day when a loud noise startles me I have a flashback of that time. Suddenly, I am in that chair in that guard house in Korea for a few seconds until my mind tells me it is really over, and we are all safe at last. Then I thank God once again.

Solitary Confinement

I think I experienced the following form of torture from January to May 1951. One morning when we were out for the lecture, we were squatted on the ground.

One of the guys said, "Why don't we get any mail? Under the Geneva Convention we are entitled to receive mail."

The instructor said, "You don't get any mail because the planes come over and bomb everything. Even the little dog on the road gets bombed."

I looked at the guy next to me and said, "I bet that little dog was pulling a 105 Howitzer [a large cannon]."

The guard behind me spoke perfect English, and I didn't know it. Unfortunately, he had heard my comment. He grabbed me by the back of the neck, spun me around, and spit in my face. When he did, I automatically kicked him. It was not the smartest thing I ever did, but it was a reflex action. But I guess if it happened again today, I would probably have the same reaction.

He dragged me up to the front of the group and put me before Communist Comrade Lim. He was the instructor who was in charge of all the instructors in Camp 5. I could not have chosen a worse day to be in trouble and be brought in front of the Comrade.

The Comrade looked at me and said, "W.W. Smith. Don't you know I could have you shot? I think I will have you shot. Get down on your knees and pray to me that I don't have you shot." Then he backed up and waited.

A peace I had never known before came over me. I took a step backward. I pulled myself up to my full height and said, "Shoot me. My religion says I pray to no man." Then I waited. Two of my buddies ran forward and grabbed me. They yelled, "Bi-oke. Bi-oke" which means, "He's sick. He's sick."

I will forever be in my buddies' debt because if it had not been for them I probably would have been shot. It took tremendous courage for these two friends to come to my rescue. That night the guards came for me, and I was taken to headquarters. That was the beginning of a really bad time for me. I should have known they would not let me get by with that kind of behavior.

I was put in a small dark room. The guard opened the door once a day and put in a small bowl of cracked corn. When the bowl was empty, they immediately took it and filled it with water. This happened only once a day, and this was the only time I saw daylight and only for a few seconds. I never heard a human voice for the entire four months I was in there.

I had to use one corner of the room for a latrine. Can you imagine the smell after that length of time? I did everything I could think of to keep my mind busy. I created hip-hop by making up a very long poem. I didn't know what hip-hop was then, but it helped. I quoted all the scripture I could remember from my childhood. I practiced biofeedback even though I didn't know that was what it was called then either.

I didn't know where I was, but I sure knew why I was there. I had been told I could come out when I decided to become a good student. That was the only part I was worried about. I knew I would never change my mind, so I was prepared to die there.

From the day of my capture I had expected to return home, but at this point I looked at myself as a dead man. I had a peace about dying. I guess God just gave me peace not to worry.

I have been asked how I had the courage to stand up and say "Shoot me," and I have always replied, "When your turn comes, the words will be given to you, and you will feel the peace I felt that day in Korea." At that point in time it didn't make any difference. I was ready either way. I just felt God put His hand on me, and I knew His peace.

One day the door opened wide and the guard said, "W.W. Smith, come."

I could not believe it was over. I was still not a good student. I guess they just got tired of waiting for that to happen. The guard had to help me back to the hut. I could hardly walk or talk, and I could not see at all.

It took at least two weeks before I began to feel anywhere close to normal. The guys in the hut had to lead me around for a while because I could not see. They really were wonderful, helpful, and kind to me when I returned. It was really very strange being with people again after all that time in solitary confinement.

After I returned home in 1953, I was told by the FBI that during this time I was held in an old bank vault in the bottom of an abandoned bank building. Of course I was not the only one put there, but it surely was a terrible place to be.

So many people think the prisoners in Guantanamo Bay, Cuba, have it so bad. Take a look at their conditions and ours—I don't think so.

Standing on the Ice

I don't want to make it sound like punishment happened to me every day because it did not. But punishment in one form or another was used on someone every day. When it did happen, it was the worst time of your life, and you wondered if it would be the end. Sometimes you prayed that it would be the end, it was so bad. This is what I meant when I said that we considered ourselves dead already. Every one of us wanted to live, but we had seen so much and lived through so much, and we never knew who was next to die.

The physical torture was terrible, but the body can only take so much, and you pass out. I have already said the mental torture was the worst because you can't turn that off. Even after 55 years I still have flashbacks. I wish that was not true, but it is, and there is nothing I can do about it.

Most of the punishments were given to us when we were alone, and that made them all the more frightening. The only time I was ever punished with a group was when we had to "stand on the ice" after we had been caught stealing shingles off the Chinese guard hut. I was on my way back to our hut to burn them when I was caught. I was hit with a rifle butt once or twice and taken immediately to "The Ice" on the Yalu River. I stood with the shingles over my head for eight hours. I estimate they weighed about 20 to 25 lbs., but they felt a lot heavier than that after a few hours. I kept praying to hang on and not give them the pleasure of failure. The good Lord answered that prayer and a lot more of my petitions during those long, hard days.

I feel sure that this is when my hands and feet froze. There were eight to ten of us on the ice that day in January of 1951. We were not allowed to talk. Some of the men died on "The Ice," some died of pneumonia shortly afterwards, and the lucky ones survived. After several hours out there, you become numb and don't really feel the passage of time or the cold.

47

The second time I was put on "The Ice" was for giving the Chinese instructor a smart remark about Taiwan.

He said, "Taiwan is an integral part of China, and we want it back."

I told him, "You have my permission. Go and get it if you want it."

This did not sit well, so he put me on "The Ice" for four hours so I could see the error of my ways. I had to stand at attention the entire time.

The third and final time I had the pleasure of this little excursion was when I stole some bean paste to put in our cracked corn to give it some flavor. It helped a little. We put it in the corn, and then Mendell, Red Brown, and I ate it.

I was caught because someone squealed on me. I have a good idea who the squealer was and so does he, but I will not mention him because it will look bad on his family. He may have had the courage to tell them what he did while he was a POW, but I doubt it. He knows who he is and that is enough for me.

That time I stood for six hours. I was fortunate because I survived all three times with only frozen feet and hands. Some of the guys were much worse off. Some didn't make it at all. So again I have the Lord to thank for looking after me.

Chapter 6

Some Days Were Better...

To the communists, May 1st is like our Labor Day so the Communists were feeling generous, and we were given a pig. Now mind you, it was not a very big pig, it weighed maybe only 200 pounds. That sounds pretty big until you remember about 500 men needed to eat. Then it doesn't look so big.

We decided not to look a gift pig in the mouth, as the saying goes. The eight of us who did the cooking were assigned to kill the pig and prepare it to become a meal of soup.

A British guy was in charge of the fire. As anyone who has ever killed a pig can tell you, there is a right way and a wrong way to do it. After the pig is dead, he is put into a vat of hot water to loosen the hairs from the skin, and then it is very clean. Well, the Brit left the pig in the hot water too long, and the hairs set in the skin so tight they could not be scraped off.

As a result, we had to shave the pig. We were given a knife so we could scrape the hairs from the hide. We also used the knives we had made from the shanks of our boots. By this time the

49

Chinese were very angry and knew something had gone wrong. They called the entire company out, put the British guy up front, and started asking, "What happened to the pig?"

The Brit said, "It just happens sometimes; nature did it."

The guard flew into a rage and started yelling, "Where is Nature? Bring him here. Where is Nature?"

The guards spent all afternoon looking for Nature. Apparently, the guard thought Nature was one of the POWs who was hiding or who had escaped, and he was very angry. We laughed at the guard as he looked for Nature. Finally, he was called back to the guard house without finding Nature.

After we finally had the pig shaved, it was ready for the next step. The Chinese have a very unique way of finishing the next step with the pig. They cut a small slit in the hind leg, insert a metal rod the size of a finger, and ran it through his hide. They then pulled the rod out and blew air into the hole. They wrapped the hole and tied it with a string so the air could not escape. Next they took a steel rod and began to beat the air through the hog, which separated the skin from the meat. After this was done to both hind legs, the pig was so bloated it looked like a balloon. It worked. The pig was then butchered and put into the pot for soup.

It had to feed 300 to 500 men, so no one got very much meat to eat, but the soup was warm and tasted so very good after the long months of cracked corn and millet. When you didn't know where your next meal was coming from, or when it was going to come, you took what you could get and were grateful for it.

I think the laugh we had over "Nature" was as good for us as the pig soup. Most of the time a G.I. found something to laugh about to keep his morale up. We sure needed this one.

The Sick Compound

The sick compound was a small compound within the larger Camp 5. There were five huts in the compound set in a semi-circle. Each hut had multiple rooms. We slept in one hut, the guards slept in one hut, and we cooked in another. The doctors were also in another hut, that is when we had any doctors. They did the best they could without any medicine for the men. The sick were in the other huts. The camp commander for Camp 5 was at the compound too, with his personal body guard in another hut.

It was a full-time job of cooking and cleaning, and when you add taking care of the sick, I really was a very busy fellow. I guess you could say it was a hard job, but one I didn't mind doing. I think working on the farm all those years growing up probably helped me to be prepared for the hard work I had to do in Korea. On the farm I worked from daylight to dark, and here I worked whenever and wherever I was needed.

Of course this was harder both physically and mentally than the farm and the work at home, but at least I was partially prepared for the job. Otherwise it would have been an even harder time for me. The guys who grew up in the city had a really tough time getting used to the harshness of our living conditions. It seemed to come a little easier for the ones of us who grew up in the country and had very domineering fathers (some of them almost to the point of cruelty). At the time I was going through the harsh punishments of my childhood, I didn't think I could survive them, and now I guess I have them to thank for my survival in that terrible place. Again, I can look back and see the hand of God at work in my life.

I was working at the sick compound in the summer of 1951. I stole some steamed buns from the Chinese and passed them to Joe Adams. He was our contact man from the sick compound to the camp. Anything we could steal we would pass to him, and he would give it to the sick in the main camp. We could all have been shot at any time for doing this, but the guys needed help and someone had to try.

I also stole the buns for an escape attempt for Willie Krobath and four others. I have tried and tried to remember who they were, but I can't. If my recollection is correct, I was squealed on by one of the Progressives (or "Pro's" as we called them) who collaborated with the enemy to get better treatment for themselves. Every time they did something like squeal on one of us, they received better food and favors for themselves. They would tell on everyone they thought they could without suffering any consequences.

I was called to headquarters and roughed up, which usually means a substantial beating. This depended on which guard was doing the beating. If it was a guard that liked to beat people up, the whole experience was more brutal. If you had a guard that was in a better frame of mind, then the beating was not quite as bad. You never knew. I have been beaten into unconsciousness and revived, then beaten again, and passed out again and again. You never knew how many times you came to and passed out again because you were in a state of semi-consciousness where time had no meaning.

After that was over, I went though a court martial. The court martial held by the Chinese didn't mean anything because we were not allowed to defend ourselves. It was simply a sham put on for show and used to play with our minds.

In this case I was guilty of what I was accused of doing. In most cases I was not guilty but was punished anyway. I was sentenced to nine months of hard labor and sent to the sick compound to begin my sentence. Nothing had changed except that I had been roughed up before the court martial. I was right back at the same job I had before they started, and Krobath had his buns! An escape was tried. It was not successful, but it was tried.

There were no doctors at the sick compound at this time, and we still had no medicine, but we took care of each other the best we could under the circumstances.

I was assigned to cooking duties, and my buddy Joe Ascue was assigned to the sick compound about this time. Now we were in a position where we could really help some of the others.

We had access to a little bit better food: eggs, potatoes, Chinese cabbage, grease, and cooking oil, because we used the same kitchen as the Chinese guards. We were not allowed to eat this food, but we could steal it and we did. We did get a little of it for ourselves. I learned to pick up an egg, punch a pin size hold in it, and suck the egg out without breaking the shell. I always was able to put the shell back in its place unnoticed.

Getting Fixed Up...a Little

I didn't have a bath until the Yalu River thawed in June 1951, which was eight months. That is a long time! We all had long hair and full beards by then. Our feet and hands looked like we had handled old dirty money—they were dark green.

In June 1951, the Chinese took us out and gave us a hair cut and clipped our beards. Our eyes were sunken back in our heads about an inch into our faces, and we were beginning to look like skeletons, so when the hair and beards were gone, we really looked bad.

One of the guys, Red Brown, from Orlando, Florida, came back to the hut, and the guys at first would not let him in because they did not recognize him without the hair and beard. It took awhile to convince them who he was until finally they recognized his voice. Now we have a good laugh over this at the conventions.

One of the guys swears that he threw his field jacket down at

53

this time, and it crawled away because there were so many lice in it. I did not see this happen, but I don't doubt that it was true. The lice were a little better after our bath, but not much.

Some Days Were Better Than Others

I do not intend to make it sound like every day was terrible because it was not. Of course it was terrible because we were in captivity, but we were not beaten and harassed every day. That made some days more bearable than others.

I look back on the times when we were not beaten and find a couple of stories when we would do things that would make the guards so mad.

There was a young friend of mine named Dale Reeder from somewhere in Iowa. We decided to make moonshine in the summer of 1952. This was before I was transferred to another camp.

The Chinese gave us a sugar ration three times during our captivity. It was brown, unrefined sugar. We were able to talk some of the guys into giving us their rations to lend to our endeavor. (Bean paste was also periodically given to us by the Chinese. It was in a large crock, and we were issued a tablespoonful each. And of course we stole potato peels, cabbage leaves, and pig weed to supplement our meager diet.)

Each of the guys who contributed to the ingredients was going to share in the moonshine when it was ready. We mixed our treasure, put it into a helmet, and buried it in the floor of the hut. We covered the hole with a straw mat and allowed this mixture to ferment for about three weeks. The guards could smell the liquor, but they could not find it. As I said, they were so angry.

At the end of three weeks, Dale and I could not wait any longer so we uncovered our cache of moonshine in the middle of the night. It smelled wonderful as long as you could not see what it looked like. It was the color of dark cream but had a really good taste. The guys enjoyed the party we had over the helmet that one night in Korea. We drank the liquor out of our aluminum bowls, and it sure tasted better than cracked corn and millet, even if we did make it ourselves.

Some months later Joe and I decided if Dale Reeder and I could make a little whiskey in the hut, then he and I could make a lot more if we could collect the ingredients. We decided to try.

We finally found an earthen crock about 2-1/2 feet high that would hold about two gallons. The jar was large enough in which to try our experiment. Then we started to gather the ingredients.

We again talked some friends out of their sugar rations. It was a very small amount of sugar we each had, and we didn't get it very often so it was very precious. They all decided they would rather have a good stiff drink of whiskey rather than a little sugar. I cannot remember for sure, but I think there were five others besides Joe and me involved. There would not be much whiskey for any of us, but some was better than none.

Joe and I had the opportunity to steal the ingredients, so we began to collect all we could. We stole cabbage leaves, potato peelings, corn, pig weed that grew wild, and anything else we thought would flavor our moonshine. We added everything to the crock.

Now came the hard part—finding a hiding place large enough for the crock. We walked, talked, and hunted for several days for the perfect place for our treasure. We wanted it to be close by so we could keep an eye on it, if possible. We finally decided to take the rocks out of the wall. We took the mud from between the rocks very carefully and inserted the crock in the hole. We then replaced the rocks in front of the crock and put the mud around them. We stepped back and looked at the wall. You could not see where the rocks had been moved.

Our hiding place was directly in the sun, and the solar power began to ferment our wonderful whiskey. We left the crock in place for about three weeks. I do not know how whiskey makers can let their product sit for a long time. We could hardly wait the three weeks.

The smell was wonderful and very powerful. The guards smelled it too. The guards had several shake-downs during those three weeks. They did not know what the odor was, but they knew it was strong.

Everyone was taken from the hut several times and made to stand at attention. The guards said, "Does anyone know what that smell is and where it is coming from?" Everyone said, "No, I don't know what it is!" Joe and I stood there with a straight face and said, "We don't know either."

We kept thinking the guards would figure out where the whiskey was hidden because the flies on the wall were so thick. They never put two and two together, and our whiskey was safe.

This was about the time we had to have 40 flies a day each for the Chinese. All we had to do was walk by the wall and scoop a handful off the wall, and you had your flies. By the time you would turn around, the flies had returned and the wall was black with them again. The flies were like the guards. They could smell the whiskey, but they could not find it either.

After the three weeks were up, and we could not stand it any longer, we decided to remove the whiskey and have a drink. The seven of us gathered, cups in hand, for the unveiling of our treasure.

Joe and I again removed the mud and rocks in front of the crock and took it out from the wall. We finally had our hands on our wonderful mix. We carefully removed the lid from the crock, and we all had our first look at the contents. My heart sank, but I would never let the others see.

I kept thinking, *This is awful stuff!* It was thick and the color of dark cream. I felt like some of the mud from the wall had probably seeped into the crock, giving it that color.

I decided to go ahead and have a drink. I filled my cup and took a large swallow. It was not bad. In fact, it was fairly good. Joe decided that since it had not killed me, he would try a drink. He thought it was good too. All the other fellows followed Joe but they quickly decided it was awful and did not want any more to drink. They figured they had lived through the beatings and punishments from the guards, but they might not survive our hooch.

Joe and I decided just the opposite, and our desire to drink it was more than our fear of the consequences, so we drank it all. It took us several days, but we did finish off all the wonderful whiskey even if we did have to force ourselves. After all, why should we let all our hard work go for nothing? The guards never did find our hidden treasure, and Joe and I lived to tell the tale of our home brew.

We did not know what to do with the crock after we finished with it. We finally decided to carefully replace it in the wall. I wondered what the person who tore down the wall years later and found the crock would think. I think about it sometimes and smile.

The Bell

The Chinese would call us to formation by sending a guard to each hut, but we were not moving fast enough to suit them. They did not know that most of the time the troops were slow on purpose. Most of the time all of us did anything we could to aggravate our guards. It was a little thing, but sometimes the little things can mean a lot. It was the only way we could fight back.

In the spring of 1951 the Chinese decided they needed a

better way to call us to formation. One day we were outside our hut, and two men approached carrying a long hollow pipe about seven or eight feet long and about four to five inches in diameter.

The guards put up a tripod and suspended the pipe from the center tripod pole. After the pipe was suspended, the "bell" was ready. There were several problems that I could see, the main one being it was hanging right outside our hut. It sounded like a fire-bell going off when it was rung in front of our door. Another problem was that it was used not only by the Chinese, but by every G.I. who passed by and thought he could get away with setting it off. The club hung loose and was in easy reach of the pipe. No one could resist the urge to give the pipe a whack. It was just another way to harass the guards and was a very good idea unless it happened to be outside your hut.

I was trying to figure a way to get rid of the nuisance of the pipe, but the decision was taken out of my hands. Some of the guys went out one night and cut the pipe down. It took at least two men to carry the thing because it was very heavy. The pipe was immediately taken to the Yalu River. That was the last we ever saw or heard of the bell. I do not know who took the thing down, but I sure was grateful to them. The guards were furious but did not replace it, and I was so glad. They just started calling us to formation over the loud speaker. I still cannot figure out why they did not replace the pipe, but it is one of the things for which I was grateful.

Father Kaupon

I did not know Father Kaupon as a personal friend, but he was probably one of the best men I have ever known in my life. His reputation was well known in The Valley and in Camp 5. All you had to do was mention his name, and everyone knew who you were talking about.

The men who were on line with Father had stories about him and told them to all of us. One story I especially remember was of Father riding a bicycle in the combat zone as he moved from place to place, giving communion to the men and praying with them no matter who they were. No one seemed to know where the bicycle came from, but the rumor was it was confiscated from a North Korean on one of our big pushes north.

The first time I came in personal contact with Father was on a very, very cold hill in The Valley in 1950. He was in a hut with the sick and wounded, and when I opened the door to the hut, I was very shocked to see how badly beaten Father was.

I left the food with the sick, wounded, and Father, and then returned to my hut. I saw Father later in Camp 5 a few times, and then I think he was moved to the officer's camp, but later he ended up at The Temple when it was the temporary hospital.

Father was a Catholic priest, and he was also a wonderful human being. He had time for everyone—Catholic, Protestant, Jew, or anyone who needed him. He had encouragement for all and blame for none. The Communists were afraid of him because his influence on the troops was so great. He did not have to say anything. All he had to do was to be in camp to be an influence. I am sure he went hungry many days because he shared his meager food with the very sick. He only received enough to barely survive, but still he shared.

One incident, I remember vividly, happened on a burial detail. It may sound terrible to you, but to me it only made Father an even greater man. We had a body between us. Father was praying at the G.I.'s feet, and I was at his head. I glanced up. I was trying to get the guys field jacket off, and Father was taking off his socks. I dropped my head, bit my lip, and said, "Thank you, God, for this good, good man." We both continued to steal clothes. We had to bury all bodies naked. They didn't need the clothes, but we did because we were freezing to death by the hundreds.

When the guards brought Father to The Temple, I was working there. He had been badly beaten and was put into a small room. The Chinese put a bowl of cracked corn by the door, just out of Father's reach. He was too weak to get to the food, and they forbade us to hand him the food, to help him, or to speak to him. He died in that room all alone. They never told anyone where they buried him. They were afraid of him even in death, so we don't even know where his body is.

The Communists Couldn't Stop Us

We were not allowed to do anything religious, but that did not stop us from trying. We would slip from one hut to another and have a religious service. There were usually eight to ten of us. You had to be careful because not everyone could be trusted, unfortunately, not even about religious services. It was always sad when one of our own could not be trusted, and said and did things that got others hurt, just to get better treatment for themselves.

Even the thought of getting caught did not stop us from having a service. I do not know what they would have done to us if they had caught us, maybe put us to death. I was told that later the Communists allowed the freedom of religion, and put a cross on the hill above Camp 5. I can't say this from experience, but a friend who returned told me it was true. The Communists could not stop religion, so they decided not to try. Their whole system is based on atheism. This was another reason they were so afraid of Father Kaupon. He had spiritual power they could never understand.

There was another man in Camp 5, who helped me a lot. He was a professor at UCLA. I wish I could remember his name, but I can't. We would gather in a hut to listen, and he would begin to tell us stories about books he had read. He would keep our minds busy, and the stories were very interesting. As I said, you learn to do a lot of things to keep your mind busy.

I remember seeing him when he had been brought out of The Hole. I never knew why he had be put there in the first place. He was dirty and disheveled and very tired. I never knew what happened to him, and I never saw him again.

That was another of the techniques the Chinese used on us. They took away people, and you never saw them again. They usually were taken in the middle of the night. That is why the mental torture is far worse than the physical. And that is why we were so hungry for the spiritual—because it could ease both.

Chapter 7

Brainwashing

The Korean War was the first time in history that the brainwashing technique had been used on any soldier. When it is used correctly, it is a very effective tool, and believe me, the Chinese knew how to use it.

The Chinese began by reducing the men to the animal stage. This was part of the psychological problem of not knowing what was going on around you. You were stripped of everything, and you had no control of anything. I can't really explain how it feels to be that vulnerable. You can only wait for the next order. It is very difficult especially for Americans who are used to making their own decisions and being in control of their lives.

Even in the Army we still have some control over our lives, but in captivity we had none. I felt out of control, which I was. I felt so lost and lonely even in the middle of all these men. That was the way the Chinese wanted us to feel. We had to fight it. I never let them succeed with me. They wanted to keep us thinking about home so we would be vulnerable and easily molded. I tried to keep my mind busy and not dwell on home.

Of course we could not entirely help thinking of home and family. I was concerned about my situation and how her worry about me would affect my mother. I knew it would be very hard on both her and my paternal grandmother. I knew they would be praying for me every day, but I also knew they would be worried.

I was so glad I was not married at the time of my captivity. It was bad enough to worry about my mother and grandmother. If I had a wife, it would have been so much more difficult. I just had to put the thoughts of home out of my mind the best I could so the Communists could not get to my mind. I had to keep my mind busy and not dwell on home, or they would win after all.

These were the steps they took to brainwash us:

1. Give only enough food to keep the human body alive.
2. Give only enough shelter to keep the human body from freezing to death.
3. Segregation by rank and nationality
4. No medical treatment
5. Reactionaries (troublemakers) segregated again

After all these things were tried, some of us still didn't respond but continued to harass our captors in every way we could. We were singled out for all the punishments and received harsher treatment than the general population of the camp.

One of the saddest things about the whole situation was that the Chinese Instructors were better educated than 90% of us. They all had college educations from Georgetown, Berkley, Harvard, Yale, and the best universities in the U.S. This really made me angry to see U.S. higher education used against us.

Some accounts of the Korean war say there was no such thing as brainwashing. If the author of those articles had been subjected to the techniques that were used on us, then I challenge him to talk to 100 men from Camp 5 and Camp 2 Company 3, and not the few that were interviewed in his article. It is very easy for someone who has never been there to pass judgment. The author never sat in the cold, sleet, rain, at 50 to 60 degrees below zero in summer clothes and listened to the same old line over and over again and again.

I HAD TO DO THAT!

He never sat with the hunger pains gnawing at his belly until he thought he would lose his mind, his own filth probably running down his leg from dysentery because he couldn't move since someone had a gun on him.

I HAD TO DO THAT!

He never spent a week in The Hole, sitting in the same filth, eating and drinking nothing except what his friend could steal for him and crawl out on his belly to bring it to him in the night. He never was the friend who knew if he was caught stealing, he would be shot.

I HAD TO DO THAT!

He never spent four months in solitary confinement. No human contact. No human voice. Total darkness. Total silence. Barely enough to eat to stay alive. Using part of the room for a bathroom. Even a dog will not defecate where he sleeps. Can you imagine the smell after four months?

I HAD TO DO THAT!

He never stood on the ice until his hands and feet froze. He never watched his friends drop dead from exposure and fatigue in the extreme cold, after he had been there eight to ten hours with his arms over his head.

I HAD TO DO THAT!

Brainwashing

He never slept in an 8 X 10 mud hut with 18 to 20 men, so close they had to sleep spoon style because there wasn't room to sleep any other way.

I HAD TO DO THAT!

He has never been taken to headquarters for something he didn't do and been beaten to unconsciousness, revived, and beaten again and again because someone squealed on him to get better treatment for himself.

I HAD TO DO THAT!

He has never been hung by his wrists with his feet off the floor until his shoulders pull out of their sockets, making his hands go numb with the pain, until he passed out.

I HAD TO DO THAT!

He was never set in a chair and had a gun put to his head, and heard the trigger snap. If he had time to think about the bullet, he would probably lose his mind.

I HAD TO DO THAT!

He never had the psychological pressure that came in the still of the night when he was in a small hut curled next to a man, usually a friend, because of the way he had to sleep "spoon style." He never whispered quietly in the night about home and family and talked about loved ones he has left behind, what he had waiting for him when the ordeal was over, if it is ever over, the girl he hoped to marry, the one he hoped to meet, the family he wished to raise.

I HAD TO DO THAT!

Suddenly one night, a guard stepped to the door of the hut and called a name. Everyone's heart stopped because they never knew when it would be their name. That night they took my friend. I felt relieved, but guilty at the same time. You never knew what happened to the ones that were taken out of the hut, and even now, 55 years later, I still don't know where they are.

I HAD TO DO THAT!

No brainwashing? Well, maybe no documented cases, but they sure knew how to bring you to your knees in a hurry. I don't know what name you can or should give it.

They strip you of everything, and they begin to work on your mind. It is a very hard thing to overcome and resist, especially for a young person who is sick, tired, cold, hungry, lonely, fearful, worried, uncertain, and in emotional turmoil.

It's obvious to us now that it didn't work since there were 7160 UN Forces taken prisoner in the Korean War, and only 21 Americans chose to stay in North Korea. I think that ratio is very small.

I would still like to sit down with the author of that article and tell him about brainwashing.

Chapter 8

Fellow Soldiers

I am going to take time out here and tell you about three of the people who came to mean a lot to me and one who failed in upholding his friends.

Dr. Shaddish

I had a terrible toothache and I went to see Dr. Shaddish for help, even though he was not a dentist. He really had nothing to help me with, but said he would try anyway.

I sat in a chair and laid my head back. The British doctor stood behind me with his hands on my forehead to help keep my head still. Dr. Saddish straddled me and sat on my lap. That is the way they pulled my tooth. All they had was a pair of pliers, and nothing for the pain. When the tooth came out, part of the jaw bone came with it. Now when I have my dentures made, the dentist has to make them with lead in the back gums to hold them in place.

Joe had a toothache a few days after I did, so I told him to go get the doctors to pull his tooth because it didn't hurt. I wasn't telling the truth because it hurt like hell, but I would never tell him. He needed the tooth pulled, and he wouldn't go if he thought it hurt. He went and had the tooth pulled. His face swelled, and his eye turned black and blue and swelled shut. He found a rag and tied it around his chin and head. He was hurting so bad. I knew what he was going through. He looked at me through those swollen eyes and said, "I would kill you if I could get my hands on you." I don't think he ever really forgave me for that trick, but his tooth didn't hurt anymore.

Dr. Shaddish helped us in so many ways with whatever he could use. For example, he told us to burn a stick and then cool them and the ends made charcoal, which we would then eat, and it would stop the diarrhea. It tasted awful, but it really worked.

Nearly all of us have irritable bowel problems now. Even though we have all the modern help in the world, we still have problems. The doctors tell me there is no cure, and I will probably have it the rest of my life. They think it is caused from malnutrition and parasites that we had while in Korea. I don't know what caused it, but it is still a bad thing to live with.

This part of the story you will not believe—I was there and I still have a hard time believing what I saw with my own eyes. One of the Turkish soldiers was sick and brought to the sick compound in the summer of 1951. He began to pass a worm, and with the help of Joe Ascue, Bullock, and a kid named Moore (called Mo) and myself, we finally got the task accomplished. After the worm was passed someone measured it, and it was 16 feet long. I know that sounds unbelievable, but it is the truth. This was certainly one sick soldier until he was rid of this parasite.

Joe Adams

My buddy, Joe Adams, from Portsmouth, Ohio, really came to the end of his rope one day in Camp 2 Company 3. He had been talking about an escape and some of the guys convinced him he could make a run for it, so he tried. These guys were not his friends to say a thing like that to him. The guard drew down on him while he was running and shot him in the leg. The guard could just as easily have killed him. They brought him back and threw him into a hut to die. Fortunately, he lived and eventually returned home.

Joe was one of the hard core reactionaries. That is why he ended up in Camp 2 Company 3. In my book, he was one of the GOOD GUYS. He is one of the two Joe's I speak of so often in this book. Joe Adams and Joe Ascue. You had to have people like these men in these situations or there would have been even more deaths.

Joe Ascue and I knew when we risked our lives to steal the food that Joe Adams would risk his life to see that it got where it needed to be. He was always ready to help us do anything that would keep the guards off balance no matter how dangerous it might turn out to be.

Joe was like the rest of us. We hoped we would come home, but we figured we were all dead men anyway.

Sam

There was a guy in the camp called "Sam," which was not his real name. He was a little slow and having a difficult time. Some of the guys always gave him a hard time too, and one day they decided it would be funny to get him to drink the ink they had stolen from the commander's office. They talked him into it. He was so sick that he had to be brought to the sick compound.

That was during the time I had been court marshaled and sent to the sick compound to work as my punishment. I was so glad I was there when they brought Sam in. Joe and I were there together because we were usually in trouble together most of the time. This time we were glad to be where we were.

After we got Sam to throw up, he felt better. Joe and I decided to take Sam under our wing so no one would hurt him again, and they never did. The word got out that Sam was protected by us. If he were ever to be hurt again, they would have to answer to us. He never left us after that. He was always with one or the other of us until I was sent to another camp.

I didn't see him again until I was in Walter Reed Army Medical Center in Washington, D.C. in 1953, and so was Sam. He came and sat by my bed every day. I was very sick, and it was as if Sam were taking care of me. He only left me long enough to eat. He was sick too, but he didn't seem to care about himself. He seemed more worried about me.

The army offered him a quick discharge. He was very much in love so he left to go home and get married. I did not see or hear from him again until 1998. He was always a little slow and had a hard time in his life.

Over the years, he had told his family about me and asked where I was. They didn't know but finally found me through mutual friends. When I found out he was alive and wanted to see me, my wife and I made a trip to Columbia, South Carolina, to the nursing home to see him. The look on his face made the trip worth everything. We spent the day with him and his sister-in-law, and took him out of the nursing home for lunch. He was so happy.

Even in the midst of all we went through, we formed bonds that can never be broken.

"John"

This is a story about a man whom I will call "John," although that is not his real name. I could give you his name, but I won't because his wife and children do not need to be embarrassed by the things he did in Korea. He knows who he is and so do I, and that is enough.

The incident happened in the fall of 1951. John worked for the "Pros," but was not quite as bad as the other two. He was still protected by the Chinese and received special privileges.

On one particular day, John was in charge of giving out some pre-cooked meat that had come into the camp. We were all in line for our portion. I had never had any contact with him, and for no reason, when it was my turn he reached out with a large stick and hit me on the arm.

He said, "Get back out of the way."

I had to step back and take it because he was protected by the Chinese guard that stood beside him. I did not receive my portion of the meat that day.

I said to John, "If we live to get home, I will get you for this."

I was so mad. I never expected to live through the captivity, and I never expected I would see him again, but I did both.

Years later I was in a VA hospital with pneumonia and very sick. After several days I was well enough to go to the mess hall for lunch.

When I walked in who should I see but John. All of a sudden I was back in Korea in 1951, in line for a piece of meat. There was no protective guard standing by him now, and we were on our own. Before I knew what I was doing or had a rational thought, I was all over him. I beat him all over the mess hall just as I had promised years before. I was so angry. I later learned that it took three orderlies to make me quit. They got me off and gave me something to calm me down.

Later, when my wife arrived, I learned the hospital had discharged "John" and called his family to pick him up. I guess they thought I would do it again if I saw him, and I probably would have at that time. I have calmed down over the years.

I saw him several years later at a convention, and my wife in the meantime had convinced me to live and let live. His conscience will hurt him worse in front of his family if I am nice than if I am ugly, and I do have to have contact with him.

He brought shame on himself, and I will not bring shame on his family. I do not know how he can look at me or my wife talking to his wife and not feel like the lowest creature alive, but he has to live with that, not me.

I intend on concentrating on those fellow soldiers who have blessed my life both in the camps and later after we returned home. There are so many of those friends that God has blessed me with!

Chapter 9

The Winter Is Past...Or Was It?

We had survived the horrible winter of 1950-1951 and were finally into the warmer weather. It was June 1951, a big time for us.

We had a bath,
We received new uniforms,
We had a shave and hair cut.

But, don't fool yourself, nothing else had changed. We still had:
The same mud huts,
The same food – cracked corn and millet,
The same lectures,
The same cruel guards,
The same punishments,
The same lice.

And now we had a new circumstance to deal with—FLIES. The flies were so bad at one point that the Communists would give us a small tobacco ration if we took them 40 dead flies. It was not hard to kill 40 flies. All you had to do was just pick them up. They were everywhere.

The funny part was, the Communists looked at the flies, but didn't keep them. So we went back to the compound and handed the same flies to our buddies, and they took them to the Chinese. They would accept the same flies over and over and never know the difference. This started in the summer of 1951 and happened every summer I was in captivity.

There was a magpie that wandered into the compound one day. For those of you who don't know, that is a small bird. It must not have been very healthy because I threw a helmet over it and caught it.

We were delighted because we had some meat. W.O. Moore from Statesville, Georgia, helped me kill and skin it, but he refused to eat any of it. The bird was so small it didn't have enough meat for everyone so we mixed it with pigweed and made soup. It was delicious. During our captivity I learned to mix just about anything together and make soup. There were only about five of us to eat this pot of soup, and we really enjoyed it.

Our Treatment

We could tell how the war was going by how the guards treated us. They became more aggressive, were harder on us, and beat us more viciously if we were winning on the front lines. In those times, they would hit us with rifle butts for no reason except they were mad. If we were losing the war, they would back off a little, never very much, but a little.

The Orientals, as a people, could be very cruel. I hate to make that generalization, but I found it to be true. They had very little regard for human life, and they seemed to get pleasure from the suffering of others. I would like to think this was only a few, but the prisoners in Japan found the same behavior there.

When the guards would have an inspection or "shake-down," they would come into the huts and search at different times for different things. If it hadn't been so serious, it would have been funny. Unfortunately, it was very serious.

For example, if they came looking for a knife and found one, the person they found it on was in for serious punishment. The funny part was if they were looking for knives, they would overlook everything else. They would even move bean paste, salt, and everything else, and not bother it. The next day they might come back and have a shake-down for bean paste, and they would move a knife and look for the bean paste. You never knew what they would do next. They had one-track minds.

There were civilians in camp working on the huts, and once it was reported to the guards that I had been talking to them. I do not know who squealed or why. It seemed I was always being reported for something or the other, no matter if I was guilty or not. I don't know why I always got the blame for so many things.

I was taken to headquarters and interrogated about what I had been talking to the civilians about. When I said, "Nothing," that was not the right answer, and I was beaten again. After I was allowed to rest for a few minutes, I knew what was coming. The guard said, "What did you talk to them about?" Same answer, "Nothing." Same consequence—more beating.

After awhile, they gave up. I never confessed then or at any time during my captivity. I didn't think I had done anything that I needed to confess to. I received a sham court martial and was sentenced to nine months hard labor, and eventually sent to work at The Temple after my punishment was over.

My punishment wasn't so easy. I was put in a room with a kid named Caverly. We were kept in the locked room for a couple of days, not knowing for sure what they were going to do with us. Then they came for us, and we had to clean the latrines. This was the nastiest job in the whole camp. They thought it would teach us a lesson. While we were at work, the American planes came over and started to bomb. Caverly and I threw down the buckets and ran. For some reason they never made us go back and finish the job. They moved me to The Temple. I never did know what happened to Caverly and still don't to this day.

I really don't know which place was called the "Death House" because both the sick compound and The Temple were death houses. Usually, when you went to one or the other you eventually died. You were so sick when you went there, but there was no medicine to help you. You had very little chance of getting well, so consequently most of the men died who were sent to the compound or The Temple.

Another Escape Attempt

In the summer of 1951 several of us decided we had had enough. So we decided to try another escape. We planned it for about a month and a half, and we thought we were ready. The ones who were going were Wells, Red Brown, Phillips, and myself. I wish I could tell you their first names, but we all went by last names and most of the time that is all we ever knew.

There was a small town of Korean civilians close to the camp. Near the town, logs were tied up that had been brought in from China and floated down on the Yalu River. We decided if we could each get a log and use it to float south down the river to our lines, then we would be free. It sounded like a good idea.

Lee Kyle and another man (I can't remember his name) swam up the river at night and cut seven or eight logs loose. Afterwards they returned to the camp and decided not to try to escape themselves. They were a great help to the four of us who did try.

When the freed logs came down the river on the current, we

grabbed them. We wrapped ourselves around the logs and laid down so we would not be seen against the night sky.

I was on my log and the log in front of me must have hit something. It raised up and hit me in the face, especially the mouth. It broke my front teeth off even with my gums. I just turned my head and spit my teeth into the Yalu River. The water was cold and the pain was not so bad. Mother Nature has a way of taking care of things, and I eventually grew a third set of partial teeth to cover the nerves of my eye teeth. Don't ask how that happened because I don't know. When I was in Japan after the repatriation, the dentist operated on my mouth and removed the teeth.

We floated for about five miles which took 2-1/2 to 3 hours because we stayed close to the shore. I have never felt so free. We made a bend in the river and suddenly came upon a lock and dam, which we didn't know were there. We ditched the logs and hit the ground running. We lasted about a mile until the guards from the dam caught us.

We were in for it. They knew where we had come from. They split us up and began the interrogation one by one for probably several hours. They were trying to find out who else was involved and how they had helped us with the escape. No one ever told them about Kyle or anyone else who helped us. I was very proud of that fact.

We were all very badly beaten. I don't know what the others received as punishment, but I was put in The Hole. I was there for about a week. When they took me out, I was given the second court martial and sentenced to nine months hard labor. Again, I was sent to the sick compound.

I was told I had tried to escape twice and if I tried it again I would be shot on the spot. For some reason I really believed them this time, and I didn't try it again.

I helped several of the other guys try to escape by stealing food for them when I worked in the kitchen in the sick compound. This was another good thing about working there. Joe Ascue and I had access to food we could steal.

We did what we could to help one another, and that made the time there more bearable.

Chapter 10

The Temple

Being sent to The Temple as a punishment for escape was not a bad thing. It gave me some constructive things to do for the sick men. I cooked, cleaned, fed, washed, and cared for the guys at the Temple like they were babies because they could not help themselves. They would have done it for me. I didn't mind cleaning a man's backside or wiping him off when he vomited. The hardest part was having to watch my buddies die because I did not have enough food and could not steal enough or find any medicine to ease their pain. All I could do was stay close and be there in the end.

Part of my job at The Temple was to help dig a pit. When we finished, it was big enough in which to bury an 18-wheeler. We had to have a ladder to climb down into it to work on the bottom before we were done. After the pit was done, we covered the top with rafters made of tree logs. We then covered this with branches, then dirt and rice straw. The pit was made to hold Chinese cabbage and other things. The reason it was so deep was so the vegetables would not freeze. The Chinese were very smart. They used everything they had.

A Chinese doctor finally arrived at The Temple, but he was of little use since we still had no medicine. When The Temple was full, we could handle about 50 to 60 men at one time.

We carried water on chogie sticks. These were sticks that were about six or seven feet long and about six inches around. A bucket or basket could be attached to each end to carry larger loads. You would carry these poles across your shoulders. Each bucket would carry seventy-five to one hundred and fifty pounds.

They were very primitive, but very effective and efficient. The buckets were used to carry water and later, rocks and dirt. We used these when we were digging the pit to stow the Chinese cabbage at The Temple.

I carried water on these chogie sticks for nine months while I was on hard labor at The Temple. It was a downhill trip to the Yalu River. It was not a straight downhill trip, but it was up a winding, steep path. Therefore, it was a very difficult climb back up the hill with the buckets full of water, even in good weather. The trip normally took about fifteen minutes. In really bad weather we went to the faucet near the schoolhouse which contained the operating room. This was a much better way to get the water.

Primitive Doctoring

This was about the time the Chinese started to do the CHICKEN LIVER operation on the men. It was my job, along with Little Smith, to carry the sick G.I. down to the school house. They had turned it into a makeshift operating room, if you could call it that. You can't imagine how we felt carrying our buddies down there. I never knew if I would ever see them again or not.

The premise of the surgery was: A chicken liver was soaked in penicillin, then the liver was inserted into an incision in the left side about six inches below the arm pit, and the incision was closed.

The prognosis was: The liver would draw all the poison from the body to that point, and the penicillin would kill the germs.

The outcome: So many of the men died that the operation was eventually halted. I dreaded taking them down for the operation because I knew how many were dying afterwards. They were probably going to die anyway, but that didn't make it any easier.

I am convinced in my heart, the few men who survived—and some of them are my friends today—lived only because their diet changed, and they received more to eat. After the operation they were given potatoes, rice, and Chinese cabbage, all made into soup. This alone made them better because before they had been eating only cracked corn and millet. They received better care, and they were out of the cold and nasty weather. I feel these factors made them better, not the chicken livers. The men who survived feel this way too.

Working at the Hospital

When the nine months of my punishment were over, I was returned to the general population of Camp 5. I knew it would not last long because I would be in trouble again. I was there about a week and then was sent back to The Temple to work. Trouble seemed to follow me around. I really liked the work at The Temple and the sick compound. I didn't have the lectures anymore, and I felt like I was helping someone who needed help.

We had a room where we slept that was to the side of the main room of the hospital. The doctor, when we had one there, stayed in another room. There were several of these rooms that were connected to the main room. I expect that at another time they had been used by monks.

There were two Chinese nurses assigned to the hospital. They were very hard working and a great deal of help. I knew a little Chinese and could talk to them some. One was an exceptionally beautiful woman. She had a long braid half way down her back. We were so short of supplies that the ladies would take the bandages off the men that didn't need them any longer and wash them so they could be used again and again, like the Army did in WWII. It is a wonder we all didn't die from this practice alone.

These Chinese ladies had to be in the army because they wore the uniform of the army. I know they were soldiers and only following orders, but orders or not they were still a big help, especially when we had 50 to 60 patients in the main room at one time. The Temple was approximately 1/2 mile from the main part of Camp 5. We were still in the camp, but we were not segregated by the distance. That is why they could bring prisoners through for medical treatment, and the rest of the people in the camp would never see them, like the fliers who were shot down in "Mig Alley" that we treated.

Nearby Dog Fights

Sometimes when we had a fire going and were very busy, all at once the Migs would come over and start a dog fight in the beautiful blue skies. I would have to put the fires out and then wait for the fight to be over and the planes to leave before I could restart the fires and get on with the cooking. It seemed that just getting the food ready took all day sometimes when the planes were busy.

Camp 5 was located close to the Chinese border on the Yalu River. The American fighter planes would come up from the air bases in Seoul to engage the enemy because the enemy would not go very far south to fight. We were located in a place that became know as Mig Alley.

The Russian planes would come across the border and fight as long as they could stay north of the 38th parallel. Everyone in the entire world was supposed to believe that the planes were North Korean and not Russian. The world knew Russia was supplying the planes and pilots, but if they stayed above the 38th parallel and were not shot down in American territory, the Russians could go on denying they were in the war.

I had the feeling they did not have the courage to stay and fight. Also, they knew our planes could not follow them into China. If they reached the Chinese border, they would be safe. So they turned tail and ran.

Before the American planes started home after a dog fight, the pilots would tip their wings to us. It gave us a feeling of pride. It also let us know that the government knew where we were, and that we were alive. That made us happy too.

Several American fliers who were shot down during a dog fight were brought to The Temple for minimal medical treatment. We did what we could because there was no medicine. We were not allowed to talk to them. We tended their wounds, fed them as best we could, and they were moved on as soon as possible to another camp. I don't know what happened to any of them.

Vince

I did not realize how many fellow prisoners I had come in contact with over the time of my captivity. In doing the research for this book, I found FBI records that estimate I probably had contact with as many as 1500 other prisoners through The Temple and other places. I have so many memories of them from Camp 5, but some just stand out in my memory so vividly.

Vince was from Cleveland, Ohio. We knew each other in Camp 5 where he stayed in the sick compound most of the time because of migraine headaches and other things. At the time I had never seen anyone suffer so badly with a headache. Years later, I would watch my wife suffer for 48 years with them in the same way I had watched Vince. There was nothing I could do for either of them but be there. We have since found a cure for my wife.

One day in 1952, I saw Vince sitting on a wall in the camp. He was so sick. I was sure he was going to die. I was being marched out to jail after the court martial and did not know what they were going to do with me. That was part of it. You never knew where you were going or when or if you would ever return.

The Chinese guards were marching me out with rifles, and Vince was sure I was going to be shot. I was fairly sure of it myself. I figured I had pushed my luck too far this time.

There were tears in Vince's eyes and he said, "Good bye, buddy." I looked at him and said, "Don't let these 'Pros' get you down. Keep fighting."

After the guards had marched me out of Camp 5 and I had said good-bye to Vince, I was taken down the road and put into an ox cart with Willie Krobath. We still did not know what was going to happen to us. We started north again. At least this time we were not walking.

We passed five women working in a field. We were not very close, but they appeared to be Americans. They waved at us. For some reason we both had the feeling they were nuns. We were not allowed to contact them. Years later, I talked to other people who saw them and did have contact with them, and they said they were nuns. I have often wondered what happened to them. If the Chinese were as cruel as they were to us, I can only imagine the fate of those good women.

Years later in 1972, we were in Louisville, Kentucky, at a POW convention. Someone walked up to me and said, "Vince Simmonetti and his wife Yolanda are out in the hall."

I said, "No, he died in 1952 in Korea." And I kept talking.

A buddy went out in the hall and said to Vince, "W.W. Smith and his wife Charlotte are inside."

"No," Vince said, "He was shot in Korea in 1952." He returned to his conversation with his friends.

This went on as the friend made several attempts to convince each of us that the other was really there. Finally, someone convinced me to go into the hall and sure enough, there stood Vince. We grabbed each other and hung on for dear life. We hugged and cried, and cried and hugged. We could not believe the other one had survived.

Finally, at 3 A.M. my wife, who by now had become friends with Vince and Yolie, looked at Vince and kissed him on the cheek and said, "I don't know who is sleeping where, but I am going to bed."

He reluctantly let us go, and we went to our room to rest. About 6 A.M. the phone rang. Vince said, "Is it really you? Come down here and have breakfast with us." We did. We remained close friends until his death in 1995. We are still close to his wife, Yolanda, his sons Chuck, Joey, and his daughter, Landy, and his grandchildren, Michael and Amanda. I miss talking to Vince very much.

Lady Ling

The lectures were still going strong in the summer of 1951. The Communists must have decided they needed some help because they brought in a lady psychologist from China named

Lady Ling. We were supposed to call her Comrade Ling, but I did not call anyone Comrade unless I had no choice. I hate the sound of the word and used it as little as possible.

Lady Ling was a very petite, pretty lady, and it was a pleasure to talk to her. She was very intelligent. She was not angry or belligerent with the men, although she tried her best to turn the men to Communism. That was her job, and she was good at it.

She would single out a soldier that she considered to be vulnerable and talk to him at length until she could convince him that Communism was better than democracy. I don't remember seeing her talk to anyone but Claude Bachelor. He was slightly "Pro" even before she began on him. About the time she arrived in camp, Bachelor lost his best friend, so he was in a very vulnerable state of mind, and I think she did not have a very hard time convincing him.

I saw them talking one day, and the next day I saw Bachelor walking through the camp with a book about Communism by Marx and Engles under his arm.

I passed him and said, "You really don't want to do this. You will have to pay for this when you go home."

He said, "I don't care."

I think he really meant that at the time because of the death of his friend.

Shortly after this, Lady Ling took me for my turn. She took me for a walk down by the Yalu River. We talked for about an hour and a half. She asked questions about my family: "What does your family do for a living?" and "What did you do before you came into the Army?"

All she asked me were background questions. I answered all

the questions, and then we talked about Communism and how I felt about that. Apparently, I didn't give the right answers because she never talked to me again. I can only assume I failed the Communist test, and I felt wonderful about that.

Along with bringing in Lady Ling, they also brought in several other people in the summer of 1951. I never figured out quite why, unless they wanted us to simply embrace the Chinese way of life. Some of those people were:

Monica Felton – the summer of 1951 and again in the summer of 1952. She was a reporter from England.

Allen Winningham – the summer of 1951. British reporter

Willard Burchett – summer 1951 and summer 1952. French correspondent.

These three all gave lectures and tried to convince us that Communism was better than our government. It didn't work with me any better than the Chinese lectures had worked.

Then there was Frank Noell, a photographer and POW correspondent with the Associated Press. He took pictures favorable to the Chinese, but he tried to position the troops in the picture so the background might give the U.S. Intelligence something to go on in trying to locate the camps. He had no control over what he was told to photograph, but by trying to manipulate the background he thought he might be helping in some small way.

Chapter 11

Never Going Home?

The summer of 1952 would prove to be a hard one, but a turning point in my captivity. I again found myself in trouble and would be given my third and final court martial. Of course it was like the other two, a sham from beginning to end. That was expected. This time I was really guilty of what I was accused of doing, but I didn't tell the Chinese.

I was put on trial with Ray Mendell, Bob Brooks, and Richard Wells. We were unloading a barge that had docked at Anton, China, and we began helping ourselves to beans and potatoes. We had tied the bottoms of our pants legs and cut holes in the pockets. We could drop in the potatoes, beans, or anything else we could get our hands on that the Chinese could not see. We were doing fine until someone squealed on us, probably one of the Progressives. They immediately had a shake-down, and we were caught with the food. We were trying to get it out of our pant legs, but it would not come out quickly enough.

We were sent back to headquarters for the special kind of interrogation you received after you had done something wrong.

This kind of interrogation usually left you black and blue for several days if not weeks. The next day, one by one we were taken to the court martial. I don't know what the others received as a sentence but I received:

LIFE AT HARD LABOR, NEVER TO RETURN HOME.

At this point, it didn't matter because we thought we were not going home anyway. During this time I was put in jail for two weeks and then taken to Camp 2 Company 3. This camp was a very small camp when compared to the other camps in Korea. There were about 3000 men in Camp 5 at one time or another. Camp 2 Company 3 only had 115 UN prisoners from all over Korea, so you can see the difference.

These 115 prisoners were the hard core reactionaries. The Chinese could not break us, re-train us, re-educate us, or control us no matter how hard they tried. We never quit harassing, trying to escape, or helping others to escape, taking care of our fellow prisoners, or most of all, standing up for our beliefs.

I could have done as the old saying goes, "Go along to get along," but I could not do that and live with myself. I was usually in trouble for speaking my mind. I could not let the Comrade run down my country day after day and not talk back. I also felt I had to help the others in their escape attempts. I had had my two chances and felt they deserved their try.

I never signed a confession while I was a prisoner because I never felt like I had done anything to confess to. The Chinese were big on confessions. I can say I am not ashamed or afraid to look one of my fellow prisoners in the face and call him friend because I only tried to help and not harm him.

They could not tolerate that because it undermined their authority with the troops, and they needed all the authority they could get. We finally made a deal with the Chinese. We would do the work, not cause any more trouble, and not be a discipline problem if the lectures stopped. If they let us alone, then we would let them alone. We were a lost cause anyway. Sometimes we were building roads, sometimes we were making a parade ground, and sometimes we were just moving dirt.

They told us again that we were not just prisoners of war, but that we were political prisoners as well. We had been sentenced to "life at hard labor," and they did not have to send us home when the war ended. Some days you could really believe them and that could work on you psychologically.

After we moved to Camp 2, we never saw any of the "Pro's" again. They probably would not have made it there without the Chinese to protect them.

We reactionaries were the soldiers who did everything in our power to keep our captors off balance, sometimes just a little remark like the one I made to a guard. He said, "If your God is so good, why is He letting this happen to you?" I said, "It's all right, because He's watching you." They were so used to watching each other that this nearly scared him to death. This was only a little thing, but it kept them off balance.

The following are some thoughts I had about that time at Camp 2 Company 3 in the autumn.

Fall 1952 Camp 2 Company 3

Out looking at the moon and stars – counting.
How much longer?
Laying on the grass saying,
"Are they looking at the same moon?"
How are they doing?
Hunger pains run through my stomach—
I double up and lay there, wonder about nothing.

Past midnight – The guards are standing at each corner
of the compound. They were doubled tonight.

I roll over, ease up, and walk back to the hut.
Everyone else is asleep.
I lay down and try to get some rest.
Too much going through my mind to sleep.

What day is it? Does it matter? They are all the same.

The Enemy Within

Camp 2 Company 3 was harder in some ways and easier in
others. The work was hard, but the lectures were over. We didn't
have the "Pro's" to worry about. At least we were away from the
Progressives we knew. Now we had to deal with the ones we didn't
know.

The Chinese had put "plants" into the rooms with us. They
would watch and listen so we had to be careful what we said and
did all the time. It didn't take us long to be aware of who was who.
Most of us at Camp 2 Company 3 were strangers to each other
when we arrived at the new camp. We were not strangers long.
You had to learn whom you could trust and whom you couldn't.
Your very life depended on your good judgment.

We communicated with each other through a code that only
the ones that could be trusted knew. We could make a few taps on
the table or the back of each other's hand and read the code.

I have a good friend named Jerry Francoise, who lives in
Fountain, Colorado. We had seen each other over the years at
conventions and stayed in touch. Several years ago, Jerry had a
stroke. He was able to return home, but with some limitations.
When he gets excited he has a little trouble talking. One time we
were sitting at a table at a hotel in Denver, and the room was full

of people. Suddenly, Jerry became very agitated and could not tell me what was wrong. He reached for my hand and began to tap the code on it. I looked up and sure enough there stood one of the men we always thought was a "plant." Jerry could still trust me and communicated with me even when he could not find his voice quick enough to warn me of the danger he felt was coming in our direction.

I let the man know he was not welcome at our table, and we would appreciate it if he just moved on. Jerry's wife, Dawn, and my wife did not know what was going on, and it all happened so fast we didn't have time to explain. These are the kind of wives that need no explanation anyway. These women support anything we do for our fellow POW buddies.

Taking Care of Business

The punishments were not quite as harsh as they were at Camp 5. We usually just had to stand at attention for a long period of time at headquarters. After what we had endured during the years at Camp 5, this was child's play.

Once again, I was assigned as cook—not all alone, but one of several. It seems this job, like trouble, just followed me from place to place. The Chinese came in one day and said, "We have some meat for you." It turned out to be a horse. As the cook, I was sent along with a crew to kill it and cook it. We were looking forward to having a pot of soup with meat in it.

In the group were Homer Wheeler, Arden Rowley, Gooseman, Robert Brooks, and myself. When we arrived, the horse was tied to the fence. I looked at it, and worms were coming out of the horse.

Wheeler went around to the horse's mouth, pulled back his gums, looked at his teeth, and said, "Look, Smitty, he's a young horse."

I said, "Wheeler, it doesn't matter how old he is. We are not going to buy him; we are just going to eat him."

But the worms were so bad, I wouldn't even kill him. The men already had so many parasites, they didn't need any more. The men were disappointed, but I felt the risk was too great. When I explained it to them, they agreed with me, and we felt we had made the right decision. I would have felt awful if I had cooked that horse and made one of them sicker than they were. The Chinese gave the horse to the ROK POWs. I don't know if it made them sick or not. That was not my responsibility.

I had the reputation of being a jack-of-all-trades. It seemed like everyone came to me to try to fix everything, and I would usually give most anything a good try. Some things I could fix, and some I could not, but I was never afraid to try.

One day my friend Dusty Culbertson came to me with a toothache. Dr. Saddish was back in Camp 5, so there was no one else to help. I told Dusty I would try to help. Marijuana grew wild there, and it was the only thing we had for pain. Dusty smoked it. When he was ready, I pulled the tooth with a pair of pliers. It came out so pretty. I was so proud of my work. Dusty said it didn't hurt and the pain was gone. So he was pleased with the job.

The next morning the guards came and got me and marched me to headquarters. I wondered all the way there what I had done. I could not think of a thing, but remember, you didn't have to be guilty to be punished.

They opened the door and there sat Dusty. The doctor showed me his mouth. He said "Lookie-Lookie" which means "Look. Next time you will know better." I had pulled the wrong tooth. They pulled the right one. I don't know if Dusty ever forgave me—I would have had a hard time forgiving him if he had done that to me.

The Chinese gave us each a notebook and encouraged us to write in it. They did not tell us they would be around later to retrieve them. I never wrote in mine, and I don't think many of the guys did.

There were several Englishmen in the camp, and I said to one of them named Winn, "I wish I had a small notebook that the Chinese do not know about."

"What kind do you want? What are you going to do with it?" he asked.

"I want to keep a list of as many names as I can to take out of here if I survive and go home." He looked at me a minute and said, "I think I can help you."

I saw him in a few days and sure enough he had made me a notebook. I do not know how he did it, but it was great and he did a wonderful job. It was about 3 X 3 inches and about 1 to 1-1/2 inches thick. It was large enough to make a list on, but small enough to hide. I wish I could have shown it to everyone, but I had to be careful. I still did not know which ones I could trust.

He bound it with a piece of cloth from a uniform. Where he got the glue to hold it together, I did not know. He didn't say, and I didn't ask. I had the feeling he made it some way. I was never so surprised over anything in my life, and I thanked him over and over.

I began to write as many names as I could in my little blue book. I wrote the names of Camp 2 Company 3 guys and as many as I could remember from Camp 5. I kept the book hidden in a special place in the loft of the hut. I still didn't know why the guards did not find it.

When the call came for me to leave there, I retrieved my blue book and my comb made out of a fuel tank from an American Jet.

I did not know where I was going, but my possessions were going with me. I am very lucky the Chinese did not search me and take them.

Chapter 12

Peace Talks

Peace talks were at long last beginning. The Communists told us that Jacob Milak, with the Russian delegation, proposed a cease fire in June 1951, and the participants argued over the shape of the table for six weeks. At least that was what we were told while we were in camp.

Another major point of contention, according to an article in the book, *The Korean War—Years of Stalemate July 1951-July 1953*, published by the Department of Defense for the Korean War Commemoration Committee, was the return of prisoners of war.

Both sides agreed to abide by the Geneva Convention of 1945 on this issue, even though the North Koreans had not followed it while we were in captivity. The convention called for the complete and immediate exchange of all prisoners at the conclusion of fighting. However, some of the Communist prisoners did not wish to return home, and the talks became stalemated over the issue.

President Truman, at the end of World War II, had sent all the Russian prisoners home, some against their will, and Stalin had killed a lot of them. President Truman did not wish to make the same mistake again, so he was very careful with the POW question.

The UN held 40,000 Koreans as Prisoners of War, who did not wish to be returned to live under Communism in the North. So, Truman reclassified them as "civilian internees" rather than prisoners of war, so they could eventually be released in the south. The UN began to screen all prisoners to see who wanted to remain in the south and who wanted to be repatriated.

In the spring of 1952 some soldiers, who were Communists, had allowed themselves to be captured by the UN forces so they could be put into the camps and cause major trouble. This is what I have said all along. You never knew who you could trust and who you couldn't. You never knew who was a "Pro" and only put in your squad to watch you, tell what was going on, and cause trouble. You had to pick your buddies to watch your back, and you had to watch theirs. Most likely your very life depended on your being right. Sometimes, it truly was a matter of life and death.

Even with all the problems, the screening continued, and in April 1953 the UN announced the results. Only 70,000 of the 170,000 civil and military prisoners held by the UN wished to return to North Korea or China. This was a big embarrassment to North Korea and China.

When you consider that we had only 21 out of 7245 POWs who wanted to stay in North Korea, I guess our percentage was not so bad. I am still ashamed of the 21 and feel they are traitors to this country and should be treated as such.

The armistice talks became stalemated again over the POW question in the spring of 1952. This meant another winter in captivity for my friends and me. It was easy for the negotiators to just keep talking. They were warm and dry at Panmanjom. We had to endure another winter of hardship—being cold and hungry, with many dying. It seemed nothing had changed.

Eisenhower was elected president, and the Communists were more afraid of him than they had been of Truman. He was a five-star general and was very hawkish on the war. They thought he might want to just go in there to end the whole thing and decide to win it.

On April 27, 1952, the negotiations began again. The Communists expressed a willingness to let the POWs decide their own fate. They quickly decided to exchange the sick and wounded, and Operation Little Switch was begun.

Little Switch
6670 Communist Troops
684 UN Troops [3]

Big Switch
75,823 Communist Troops [4]
12,733 UN Troops
(3597 American POWs included in this number)

The prisoners who decided not to be repatriated were put into a temporary camp at Panmanjom. Their respective countries could come and interview them to see if they had been coerced into staying with their captors. They were again given the opportunity to choose repatriation. When the prisoner had been interviewed again by the representative of his own government, under the supervision of a five-member Neutral-Nations Repatriation Committee, they were again free to choose what they wanted to do: go back home or go with their captors.

The truce tents of Panmanjom, called Freedom Village. This array of tents is all that marked the boundary to freedom. On one side were North Korean troops and on the other were American troops.

The Camp at Panmanjom

359 UN Personnel
10 Returned Home
2 Neutral Third World Country
347 Decided to live among the Communists[5]
(This included 21 Americans who chose to stay in
North Korea.)

22,604 Communist Soldiers
628 Returned Home
21,978 Remained in South Korea and Taiwan
25,000 Rhee, freed in June (roughly)
46,000 Refused Repatriation (approximately)[6]

This was one of the best testimonies that Communism didn't work because so many didn't want to return to live under that system.

The American stand on the prisoner's right to choose their fate was, "Do they stay with their captors or do they return home?" This one small question and the American stand on it caused the war to drag on for 15 more months. There were 125,000 more American casualties and 250,000 Communists casualties during those 15 months.[7]

I don't know if it was worth it or not. That is for the politicians of this world to decide. I can tell you this: The last year in our captivity was hell, and I have to wonder if it was worth so many lives to set a principle. Does it really matter who is right or who is wrong? Communism was stopped in Korea, and that is right, so I guess it was not all in vain.

America, the Republic of Korea, and eighteen other nations under the UN flag had secured freedom for millions of South Koreans. The armistice was signed on July 27, 1953. The war was over, at least the fighting had stopped. Bob Erickson played TAPS.

We still have forces on the DMZ because we only had a cease fire and not a peace treaty. So let's pray we all keep cool heads, and we don't have to go back and fight this war again as we have had to go back and fight in Iraq again. I pray this will not happen, but the Communists will not stop until they achieve their goals. We must be ever vigilant and prepared.

Operation Little Switch

We did not know it at the time, but Operation Little Switch had begun. Our lives were about to change again—this time, for the better. We really were going home.

Little Switch was just that. The exchange of a few sick and wounded UN prisoners for a great number of North Korean and Chinese soldiers.

This was worked out in the peace talks at Panmanjom. Little Switch took place April 20, 1953 to May 3, 1953. The numbers speak for themselves. 6670 Communist troops returned for just 687 UN troops. These were troops from all over the world, not just America.

Little Switch Panmanjom
April 20, 1953 — May 3, 1953
Exchange of Sick and Wounded

Allied Repatriated
5194 North Koreans
1030 Chinese Military Personnel
446 Civilian Prisoners
6670 Communist Troops

Communist Repatriated
149 Americans

471 South Koreans
32 British
15 Turks
1 Philippine
2 Canadian
6 Columbians
5 Australians
1 South African
1 Greek
1 Dutch
684 UN Troops

The ratio of exchange was 10 to one Allied troops for Communists troops.

The Decision That Saved My Life

I had been very sick just before the beginning of Operation Little Switch, but I did not realize it. I was later told how sick I really was by my good friend Dallas Mossman. The Chinese came around in late April 1953 and told the guys they needed a list of the sickest, and that they were to be sent to the hospital.

Dallas told my wife years later that it had been so tempting to put his own name on that list, but he knew if he did, I would die. Besides it was the right thing to do to put mine on the list.

My wife says she knows how much she loves me and how much our lives have meant to each other and if Dallas had not put my name on that list we would not have had this life together. So she loves Dallas in a very special way and will always be so grateful to him.

Of course he did not know if he was doing the right thing or not. They told him I was going to the hospital. They could have been going to shoot all the men who were sent out. My friends just had to take the chance. I was so sick that I was going to die if he didn't do it. This way I had a fighting chance. As it turned out, it was the right decision and saved my life.

Shortly before our names went on the list, the guys were told we would not be going to the hospital but would be going home. Then the temptation for my friends to add their own names was even greater, but none of them did.

There were four names put on the list. We did not know anything about the list at all. The four on the list were: James Coogan, Willie Krobath, Clifford "Little" Smith, and W.W. "Bill" Smith.

One morning the guard came in and said, "You are going to the hospital." My first thought was, *Yeah, sure.*

We collected our meager belongings and said good-bye to our buddies. I never expected to see them again. We were sick, almost as bad as some of the guys on the march, and we all knew what had happened to them. I fully expected to be taken out and shot.

We were put on a truck and taken to the officers' camp. This was our first step south. We didn't know it, but it was also our first step toward home. We stayed one day at the officers' camp, and that night they had a big dinner with lots of food. But our stomachs could not take it, so we could not eat it.

A Chinese General stood up and said, "You will soon be FREE. You are going HOME!"

Again, I thought, *Yeah, sure.*

We were given a gift. I was given a green Jade Chinese Cabbage figurine. It was broken into a hundred pieces on the way home. I still have the pieces, but it could never be fixed.

We left for Pyoktong with the officers that were to be repatriated with us. There were two of them—one was as sick as we were, but the other one was not very sick. He had only been a prisoner for about six to eight weeks. Some of the returnees looked very good, and I think this was done on purpose so we all would not look so bad to the press that the Chinese knew would be waiting for us at Panmanjom.

When we arrived in Camp 5, we were not taken to the main camp, but put into mud huts outside the camp. We stayed there about two to three days. I had been looking forward to seeing my buddies in Camp 5, but that was not to be. I was really disappointed in not being put back in the camp, but some of the guys found a way of contacting me anyway.

The Letters

The men who were going home from Camp 5 were brought to the collection point with the rest of us. I do not know who brought the sick and wounded up to us. But whoever it was, recognized me, went back to the camp, and told them I was there.

Someone came and said, "Would you try to take some letters out for us when you are released?" I did not even have to think about it. I replied that of course I would.

He went back to the camp and a lot of the guys hurried and wrote home. He came back and had 60 letters for me. We fastened them around my waist with a belt. Some of them we put in my pant legs. Have you ever tried to keep up with 60 loose letters? It seemed to me they were all over the place, but I was very happy to try. These would be the first uncensored letters the families had had since the capture of their sons. I knew how important it was for the guys to get a letter out. I did not look at the letters, so I do not know who they were from or to whom they were addressed.

104

Along with the letters I had my little blue book of names, and I wanted to get it out so badly too. I had been working on the book for almost a year, and I cannot tell you how many names were in it. I will finish the story of the letters and the book later. But I will say I received letters from their family members after I returned home, thanking me for bringing the letters out.

Heading South

This was the collection point and more were coming in everyday. We were allowed to rest. We had a shave, a bath, and clean clothes.

I was still very sick. The doctor came and put a shot of adrenalin into my heart just before we left Camp 5. I had the letters in my belt, and I pushed them under me to safeguard them. This is not the last time they would be in jeopardy before I reached freedom.

Finally, we were again headed south to Pyongyang and Panmanjom. I was still curious and apprehensive. I did not believe I was going home. I would not believe it until I was in American hands at Freedom Village. Remember, it was not so long ago that I had been sentenced to: LIFE AT HARD LABOR. NEVER TO RETURN HOME!

As we were traveling south, I became sicker and had to be put on a litter. We stopped at a farmhouse around noon to rest. We were all taken off the trucks and the litters. When the rest time was over, some of the men began to load the truck. The guard looked around at me and said, "Leave him."

There were about five or six of us who were to be left in the farm house to die all alone or be shot when the others were out of sight, like the men on the march.

The G.I.s on the ground refused to be loaded, and the ones on the truck jumped off. I think they were led by my good friend Beck from Wheeling, West Virginia. Thank God for friends. The guard became very angry. He sent for the doctor, who came into the farmhouse and put another shot of adrenalin into my heart. It worked, and I felt better. I was able to be loaded, and so were the others. The men agreed to load too, and soon we were on our way south again.

We were still gathering people along the way, and our number was growing. Later that night we arrived at Pyongyang. Most of the G.I.s were put in the schoolhouse for the night, and the sickest were put into tents. The next day we were closer to Panmanjom.

I was still having problems, and the doctor returned for a third time and injected my heart with adrenalin. I do not know who the doctor was, but he was traveling with us. He just appeared and took care of me. After every shot I seemed to feel a little better for a little while.

I do not know why he did not find the letters and book. I guess it never crossed his mind to suspect that I was carrying anything. I pushed them as low as I could down on my stomach and put a lot behind my back and in my pant legs. I do not think they would have done anything to me, but I sure did not want him to find the letters or book and take them away. He gave me the shot and walked away. The letters were safe again, and I gave a sigh of relief.

After we left Pyongyang, we were taken closer to Panmanjom. We were put into a field tent, and we would remain there for several days until we were called for the exchange.

Again, I became very ill. I think the Chinese were afraid I would die before I could be exchanged, and I was now valuable to them because they could get 20 prisoners in return for every one of us. It was in their best interests to keep me alive if possible. I

This is the final bridge to Panmanjom—the bridge of no return. When we crossed this we were in Freedom Village at last!

Picture courtesy of Arder Rowley

had come too far to be allowed to die now. They decided I could die after I got into American hands.

We were all ready and waiting in great anticipation for our turn, but the day would end, and we would not be called. We remained in the tent overnight. The next day we did the same. Prepare, hold our breath, and wait. I remained very sick. The doctor came and put another shot of adrenalin into my heart. He did it immediately before our names were called, and we were ready to go. As before, it helped and I began to feel better. We were taken out of the tent and put into an ambulance.

Starting Home

At last I was on the final road to Freedom Village. It was my turn to be released along with the 40 others in my group. I had started HOME! I could not believe it was going to happen. I would not let myself believe it until I was in American hands.

The ambulance was full, but they decided they could get one more in. So they took me off the litter and practically stood me up and then shut the doors behind me so that we were packed inside. We arrived at Panmanjom about noon on April 23, 1953. We were finally at Freedom Village!

They opened the ambulance door, and I fell out like a jack-in-the-box and hit the ground with a thud. There was a young Marine— I later learned his name was Bob Erickson from Quincy, Illinois—who picked me up off the ground, half carried and half walked me to the next man in line. The two soldiers helped me. With their help I walked into the tent. I was so sick they wanted to put me on a litter.

I said to them, "I walked into captivity, and I will walk out. Only this time I need your help to do it."

I made them let me walk. I felt like I had walked into captivity, and with the help of God and the strong arm of Bob Erickson and some wonderful G.I.s, I would walk out of captivity, and I DID.

In 1988, we moved to Quincy, Illinois, to be near our daughter and her family. I belonged to the Korean War Veteran's Association and so did Bob. At a meeting we began to compare notes about our experiences in Korea. I was telling the story of my repatriation, and all at once Bob looked at me and said,

"I remember you. I picked you up off the ground when you fell out of that ambulance at Freedom Village."

We could not believe our paths had crossed again after 35 years and so many miles! I can never thank Bob enough for the kindness he showed a perfect stranger that day so long ago. He has become a great friend.

Down the Line to Freedom

There were American and North Korean soldiers sitting at a table in the tent. You went down the line and stopped in front of each one of them. They checked us through and tagged us. I had more tags on me than a suitcase that had been around the world. I never saw anything as beautiful as those G.I.s. Seeing them was unbelievable! I was really FREE, FREE, FREE!

I began to shake and was so dizzy that a Catholic priest took hold of me and helped me sit down. I think the priest took the letters and book from me. I really do not remember who took them or what happened to them after they left my hands. I was sure they would be safe now that they were in American hands. I do know now that they were mailed.

I did not know what happened to the little blue book. When the Army officers started my debriefing in Japan shortly after my repatriation, they mentioned the book and the names in it. No one ever said, "Thank you for getting the names out." You do not do these kind of things for thanks, but it would have been nice to know right away that the book was safe. I only found out by accident when the officers mentioned it.

After we passed through the first tent, we were put into a building, stripped, and sprayed with DDT. (That was before they knew it was bad for you.) We were put on tables and given cursory exams to check for broken bones, cuts, or obvious injuries. Then we were fed. At least the food was put in front of us. No one could eat. I remember they had rice pudding, but I could not eat anything.

Later we were moved to a helicopter and started toward Seoul. We arrived about 5 P.M. This was the first day of my release.

Chapter 13

The Beginning of Freedom

We spent the night in a building that was an old silk mill. It had been converted to a hospital to receive the returning POWs. "Little Switch" just happened to be the first to come through. The next morning we left Seoul for Japan. We were taken from Kempo Air Force Base in Korea to Tokyo General Hospital.

It seemed as if things began to happen very fast at this point. We were fed several times a day. It was difficult to eat, and even more difficult to keep it down. I weighed 193 pounds when I left Japan in 1950, and I weighed 82 pounds when I returned April 24, 1953. It is very difficult to imagine a man 6 feet tall weighing 82 pounds.

The Japanese operator set up a call to my mother. We talked for a few minutes, and I told her I was all right and would see her soon.

The psychiatrists soon arrived on the scene and began to talk to us. They called the sessions "interviews." The interviews with the doctors eventually came to an end, but the ones with the FBI

111

This picture was made in Sasebo, Japan in 1949. It was the last picture taken of me before I went into combat. I weighed 193 lbs and was 6 feet tall.

This picture was taken in Tokyo after about three days of freedom. Here I am in heavy pajamas and robe, looking like a different man and weighing only 82 lbs.

and the CIA would begin very soon. They began in Tokyo in the hospital, and in my case, would continue for 16 years. They still come to the conventions for information.

Two or three days after our repatriation at the hospital in Tokyo, the FBI agents of the U.S.A. came into my room. This was nothing new so I was not surprised. The agent handed me a sheaf of papers to read. I began to read and could not believe what I was seeing.

The papers said, "Do not talk about your captivity or anything that was done to you over there, or anything that was said to you over there. If you do, you will be eligible for court martial and all the penalties. If you do not sign these papers you will not be allowed to board the plane for home."

I was so stunned. We all signed, of course. It was not a confession, but it sure made me feel bad at the time, and it certainly felt like a confession. I would not have said anything even if I had not signed the papers because I still had friends in that Hell Hole, and I did not know how long they would be there.

I did not talk about my experiences for many years until I got the clearance to speak to the Kiwanis Club in Bluefield, West Virginia. Even then there were restrictions. After the Freedom of Information Act, I received a copy of the papers. I then was free to begin speaking of all the atrocities that were committed against me and my fellow POWs.

When we were ready to leave Japan, we were put on a plane and headed for Guam. We landed on Guam and had breakfast. Next was the leg from Guam to Hawaii. We landed in Hawaii at Hickham Air Force Base and were taken to Tripler Army Hospital. It is a beautiful, pink building on a hill overlooking Honolulu.

After we landed in Hawaii and were taken to Tripler, we were put on the ward to rest and eat. We were to rest for a day and night, before we began the rest of the trip.

On the second day, a sergeant and I were taken to the library and told to wait. The orderly who took us to the room said, "Relax, General O'Daniels wishes to speak with you."

After the orderly left, we looked at each other and wondered what we had done now. Almost immediately, the general entered the room. We both stood and came to attention. He said, "At ease. You are here because you were in several camps in North Korea and there is a possibility you may have information about a Lt. Thomas Kilby from Alabama. He is my next door neighbor, and naturally his parents are afraid for him, especially his mother. We thought maybe the two of you could tell me if you had seen him or if you had heard anything about him."

I really didn't know anything about the lieutenant and neither did the sergeant. Even if I had known I wouldn't have told him, because I was thinking it might be a trap because of the papers I signed in Japan. How could we know for sure?

By the time the General was done with us, the bus taking the men to Hickham Field for transport to the U.S. had already gone. The General, his aide, who was a major, the sergeant, and I left Tripler in the General's staff car and were taken to Hickham Field in time to make the flight. That was the last I ever saw of the general. I always wondered what happened to him and the sergeant.

The final leg of the long flight was from Honolulu to Travis Air Force Base, California. We stayed a day or two at Travis and then flew to Lowery Field, San Antonio, Texas.

Several of us began to feel better. We had been kept on the ward so the public and the press could not get to us. After we reached San Antonio, Texas, most of us began to feel better. We were allowed to go into the mess hall for a meal. We went in with our pajamas on. The mess sergeant came over to us and said, "I am tired of you guys coming in here in your pajamas. I am not going to serve you. You will have to go back to your rooms." They were ordered to feed us in bed. After what we had been through for this country, can you imagine how it made us feel that a lowly mess sergeant could talk to us that way and get away with it? BUT HE DID!

I was very hurt and angry. After the run in with the mess sergeant, three of us—Mooreland, Cotton "Eyed" Joe, and my-self—decided we would not fly anymore. We decided to travel by train the rest of the way home.

We did not know that the FBI agents would be traveling with us, but as we boarded the train, Mooreland recognized one of them. They did not speak to us nor bother us in any way. They were just there. Someone said later it was for our protection, but I still wonder why they were there. We separated as we traveled East, and I never saw the other two guys again.

Sometimes I felt, *When I was in prison I knew who the enemy was, and when I came home, I sometimes began to wonder whom I could trust.*

Not to be able to talk about my captivity was very difficult. I think after I received my release in 1968 and could talk, it be-came easier. I did not feel like I had to be so careful about what I said all the time. It was a very difficult situation for a while, but it worked itself out.

It was very hard to return to civilian life after the ordeal we had been through. The Army said they were trying to protect us, but I wonder. Some of the time we felt like we were in prison camp again because we were watched over so carefully. They said it was for our protection.

We had only seen and heard what the Communists wanted us to see and hear of the outside world for 2-1/2 years, so it was a shock to try and absorb all that had happened in that time.

Inconsistencies of the 50s

The Army of the 1950s was entirely different from the Army of today. That made returning home difficult for many of us.

I was from Rockingham, and Bullock was from Fayetteville, both towns in North Carolina. These two cities were about 80 miles apart on the map, but worlds apart in their thinking in the 1950s on lifestyle.

It was unheard of for a white man and a black man to be friends, but that is just what Bullock and I were—friends. We had lived together under the worst circumstances two men ever endured and lived to tell about. Whether we were black or white did not matter. In the hell hole we had been in during the winter of 1950, the only thing that mattered was your own survival and the survival of your buddies.

One time I was working at the sick compound on hard labor, and two black men arrived. I did not know if they were on hard labor or not. They did all the same jobs I did and then some. They were given the worst jobs in the compound and were virtual slaves to the Chinese. Their names were Moore and Bullock. I was friends with Moore, but I worked with Bullock more and became closer friends with him. I can't tell you their first names because in the army we only used last names. The two of them were the best men you would ever want to know under any circumstances, and under ours they were really great men to have on your side. They did their work willingly, cheerfully, and without ever a complaint or a grumble.

I remember seeing the two of them cleaning the latrine, the worst job in camp. I always thought the Chinese took the contents of the latrines and sold it to the farmers for manure to put on the fields because it sure smelled bad around the camp in the spring when they were planting the fields. I also remember seeing them take the dirty bandages, wash and dry them, so they could be used again. This was another dirty job, but again no complaints. I worked with Bullock and Moore until my third court martial in the spring of 1952, which sent me to Camp 2 Company 3.

Bullock came out of Korea on Little Switch the same as I did, but I did not see him in the transfer from Korea to the States because he was with another group. We then met again in Fayetteville in 1953 at Ft. Bragg. We decided to spend some of our liberty time together "off base" in downtown Fayetteville. We were stopped by the local deputy sheriff. He took me aside from Bullock and said, "Don't you ever be seen in Fayetteville with that n---- again." I was speechless! He took me back to where Bullock was waiting and then he said, "Get into that car, both of you, and leave Fayetteville, and don't ever come back." We got into Bullock's car and returned to base. Neither one of us could believe what had just happened.

I was so angry to think of all the things we had been through together to be told we could not go to town and have a beer together. I could not believe it, but in the South in 1953 it was not done. So no matter the circumstances or our friendship, we could not enjoy one another's company in town.

When I married in 1955 I told Charlotte the story of Bullock and asked her if she would have any problem with a black man coming to our home.

She immediately said, "No, I will not have a problem with any man who was your friend in Korea coming to our home."

I never saw Bullock again after the night at Ft. Bragg. I have wondered over the years what happened to him and Moore.

Chapter 14

At Home

Mother never talked much about the years of my captivity. They were too painful for her. Most of the time the two stories— the one I remember from Mother, and the one published in the newspaper—don't parallel very well. According to the newspaper, Mother had been notified on November 20, 1950 by telegram that I was missing in action. The telegram came from the War Department, and I understand it was mailed to her. I remember Mother telling me the telegram said I was killed in action. I never saw the telegram, so I can't say for sure what was in it. I only remember what Mother had told me.

On November 21, 1950, Mother received a letter written by me on November 1, 1950, the day before I was captured. Mendell and I had been resting that day when the company clerk came by and said, "The mail is going out in about 30 minutes. If you want to send a letter home, get it ready."

Ray looked at me and said, "Smitty, maybe we better write home. We may not have time later." I said, "You are probably right." I wrote to the folks, and Ray wrote to his wife. We did not know how true Ray's words would be. This was shortly after the liberation of Pyongyang.

The next morning, November 2, 1950, when we were captured, we were at the farthest point north in MacArthur's push. We were 15 miles from the Manchurian Border, according to the newspapers.

I do not remember how long we were prisoners before we were allowed to write home. Mother said she received five letters from me during the time I was a prisoner. I was very careful what I wrote because I knew the letters would be screened, and only the ones they wanted to let out would make it home.

I wish I could remember how many letters I received while I was a captive, but I can't. I think there were three. I remember one in particular and when I received it. The comrade said, "This letter is 18 months old. It is being delivered through the International Red Cross. See how much they care about you?"

I don't know where it had been, The Netherlands or some place. I told him, "That's all right. It got here didn't it?" This made him very angry again.

My Name Is on the List

On December 18, 1952, the Korean government released the names of 3193 prisoners and missing in action. My name was on that list. Mother received a second telegram the same day—the one that said I was alive—but she had already heard my name from the television.

The second telegram was delivered by Mr. Watkins, our mailman, to our house in Wolf Pit outside Rockingham. One story has it that he stopped on the way to the house and picked up a neighbor because he was afraid of what was in the telegram and that it could be a shock to Mother.

I heard that she was so shocked that she had to be hospital-ized with a slight heart attack. Mom and Dad are gone now and so are my older sister Jewell and younger brother H.B. The only family I have left is my sister Wanda, and she was only nine years old when I came home.

I can only rely on the recollection of what my mother told me of the way she was notified. I talked to my Aunt Orene, who is very close to me and another one who was praying for me daily, to find out how they were notified of my release. She said the news media was full of rumors of an exchange of prisoners called Little Switch. All the family had the radio and television on night and day in case I might be in the exchange. Sure enough my name came across the screen. Orene saw it and started calling everyone, and that is how they knew I was free. The government never notified my family.

We were released on April 23, 1953 about noon Korean time. On Sunday the Japanese operator called mother at 10 P.M. and told her to stand by that I would be calling. At 10:45 P.M. Rockingham time, 1 P.M. Monday Tokyo time, I heard my mother's voice. I was in Tokyo General Hospital.

I told mother I was O.K. and only wanted some good food. She didn't need to know I had 310% disabilities. She didn't need any more worry or stress. They told mother that a group of 64 pris-oners would leave Tokyo for Guam and should arrive in Ft. Bragg about May 5-6.

I did arrive in Fayetteville, N.C. on May 7, 1953. The Atlantic Coast Lines train was due at 9:25 and arrived at 9:50. As I said in another part of the book, the FBI agents and I arrived in good order. (These were the agents who traveled from Texas on the same trains with us.)

There were about 50 people at the train station, but the main person I saw was my mother and then my grandmother Smith.

They were the two women I felt praying for me every day I was gone.

NOW I KNEW I WAS HOME!

I would not accept a parade, gifts, or anything from the community. I was just doing my job, and I didn't want a fuss made over my homecoming.

Major Ivan Cooper, my company commander in Korea, was at the station to meet the train. He told me there were 32 men missing or wounded in the battle of Unson from our company. It was very nice to see him again.

I was at home one week, when I became ill and had to go to Ft. Bragg to the hospital. I was home, but I still had a long hard road back. I just didn't know it yet. I would find it out soon enough.

Some of the hardest times I had came shortly after I returned home to rest and recuperate. After the sessions with the psychiatrists and FBI at the hospital in Tokyo, I thought I could just go home and rest, but that was not to be.

I had been home about two weeks when my parents, some family members, and I were sitting in the front yard of our house in Rockingham. It was a beautiful Sunday afternoon. We had just finished another one of my mother's southern home cooked meals. It was about 2 P.M., and everyone was relaxing and catching up on family.

A large, dark car turned into the private road that led from the highway to our house. None of us recognized it. When the car stopped, a man and woman stepped out. They introduced themselves as Mr. and Mrs. Kilby, the parents of Lieutenant Thomas Kilby. (This was the lieutenant that General O'Daniels had asked the sergeant and I about when we were in Tripler Hospital in

Honolulu.) The general kept the parents informed of the where-abouts of any returning POW that might have come in contact with Thomas. They were traveling all over the country, trying to find someone who might have come in contact with their son or know anything about him. They had come to Rockingham from Greensboro. They were on the way to Alabama, so they came by Rockingham to see me even though I am sure General O'Daniels told her I did not know Thomas.

I stood up as Mrs. Kilby got out of the car. After the introductions she asked me to take a walk with her down the road toward the highway, and I agreed. We walked and talked and cried for about 20 minutes.

She thought I knew about Thomas because the G.I. in Greensboro had told her he was sure I would know him since I had worked at The Temple. That is where they usually took the Air Force personnel, but I didn't know anything about him. Mrs. Kilby felt I knew more than I was telling her. Even if I had, I don't think I would have told her because of the "non-talk" papers we had signed in Tokyo. You have no idea how much those papers had put a great fear into me. I was afraid to talk to anyone, even to my own family.

We walked back to the house where Mr. Kilby was waiting with my parents. They thanked me, got into the car, and left. I never saw or heard from them again. I don't know if they ever found out what happened to the lieutenant or not. Eventually I heard at one of the POW Conventions from one of the guys that did know him that he died in 1951, but I don't know if the Kilbys ever found out about it.

After the Kilbys left, I sat back down with the family. Later that evening I became very ill and had to be taken back to Ft. Bragg to the hospital. I had only been home a week.

After I reached Bragg, the doctors discovered that I had

polyps in my nose. They had grown down the back of my throat on the right side and had cut off most of the oxygen supply to my right lung. They had started to grow down the left side too and the doctor said if they had grown enough to shut off the oxygen supply to the left lung, I surely would have died. They explained this as a phenomenon of nature to cut off part of the oxygen, because the lungs are too weak to do their job. They tell me these polyps were put in a jar of formaldehyde in the doctors office in Ft. Bragg. I don't know if that is true or not. I only know it saved my life when they were removed.

The FBI

After my release from Ft. Bragg hospital, I was assigned to Ft. Myer, Virginia, as my new duty station. I was working at the Pentagon, and I loved every minute of it.

The maps of Korea were to be looked at, the court martials prepared, and a lot of loose ends brought together. I was given the job of helping bring all of this to an end.

I was so happy to be working at the Pentagon, but it only lasted two or three days when I was walking down the hall and passed out. I was sent by ambulance to Walter Reed Army Medical Center, and I stayed there for ten months until March 31, 1954, at which time I was given a medical discharge. My 310% disabilities had caught up with me.

I was still too sick to be sent home, so I was transferred to Salisbury, North Carolina, VA hospital. I was in Salisbury for about a month. A young x-ray technician, who was practicing on my x-rays, found a spot of TB. I was once again transferred to Oten Hospital in Ashville where I stayed for the next fourteen months until August 1954.

The FBI had first contacted us at the hospital in Tokyo, Japan.

A small South Korean child sits alone in the street, after elements of the 1st Marine Division and South Korean Marines invaded the city of Inchon, in an offensive launched against the North Korean forces in that area.

We had only been free about three days. The interrogations had begun. The FBI sessions were long and tiring. They asked the same questions over and over again. I don't know if they were looking for answers or if they were looking to trip us up, or to see how far we could be pushed.

The psychiatrists came about this time too. We were talked to in groups and then as individuals. I tried to tell them everything I could. I thought something I remembered might help someone who was still over there. No matter how much you tried to help either group, it never seemed to be enough. They were never satisfied and kept coming back for more.

After we signed the papers which said, "Not to talk about our experiences in Korea with anyone except the FBI and only then with proper identification," we were told we were subject to court martial if we did talk. There were five copies. I now have copies of these papers, which I finally obtained through the Freedom of Information Act.

I knew the Communists in the U.S. would report to the Communists in North Korea. They would watch everything we did or said, and one wrong move and my friends would have hell to pay.

When I wanted to speak to the Kiwanis Club in Bluefield, West Virginia, in November 1968, I had to write to the Department of the Army Intelligence Division for a release to speak. I was granted it on November 19, 1968, but I was sent a list of restrictions that I could not talk about.

After I received my release in 1968 to talk a little more freely, I began to talk at schools, scout troops, churches, and anyone who asked me. People need to know about man's inhumanity to man and how unbelievable it really is.

If the ones of us who were there do not tell the story, the

people will never know the truth. I am trying to write my experiences so maybe we will begin to understand that although this country is the greatest in the world, it is so very vulnerable from both outside and inside our borders. We must always be on constant guard to keep ourselves free. Our freedom can slip away from us in a minute. I know because mine did. One minute I was a free man, and the next I had no control over anything. That was a horrible feeling that the people of this country must never be faced with.

The FBI came to the house in Rockingham while I was supposed to be home resting and recuperating. It seemed like there was no rest from them.

After I was hospitalized at Walter Reed Hospital, they came daily for a long time. At that time I could understand why because they were preparing the court martials for the "Pro's," which would take place very soon. They needed all the information they could find.

Finally, when I was transferred to Salisbury and then to Oten, the doctors made them stop coming because of my health and the fact that I needed the rest.

After I was released from the hospital, I went to Bluefield to see Joe. After an escapade I will tell you about later, I found a job and went to work. I met Charlotte, and we were married December 24, 1955. We lived in the apartment that Joe and Emily had lived in when I first came to town behind the big white house of Shenandoah Ave. We had been married about 14 months. Our Lisa was born there and everything was perfect for us. I had not given the FBI a thought for a long while.

One morning in early 1957, there came a knock on the door and there stood an FBI agent. We invited him into the apartment. It had started again. They asked very politely if Charlotte had some place she could take the baby and stay for the next few hours. Lisa was about four months old at the time.

Charlotte packed Lisa's clothes, bottles, and baby food, enough for a day, and prepared to leave the house. She looked at me and said, "I will take Lisa and go to Mom's." Charlotte had only to go down the stairs and across the walk to be at her mother's. That wasn't the point. The point was that she had to leave our home in the first place.

The FBI men set up their tape recorders and their typewriters in the kitchen, and the "interrogation" began. It lasted all day. They left at 5 P.M. and returned at 9 A.M. the next day. The same thing happened. Charlotte and Lisa had to leave home. Finally, after three days, the ordeal ended.

After several months the ordeal was repeated. What we didn't know was that this was only the beginning. We never had any warning. They just showed up three or four times a year and stayed as long as they wanted.

Finally, after 16 years, Charlotte had had it. The next time the FBI arrived, she came into the room and said, "Enough is enough. Please go, you have enough." They left politely. In about an hour the phone rang. The agent said, "We will be back tomorrow."

Charlotte lost it for some reason as she never had before and said to him, "No, you won't and if you do you had better bring three things: 1) Proper identification, 2) Your lunch, and 3) Three large men because it is going to take the large men all day for you to get back into my house and get back at Bill again. He has had enough."

They have never returned to this day. Charlotte has always been sorry she didn't run them off sooner, but I was trying to help and be a good citizen and still be a good soldier. But I guess as she said, "Enough is enough!"

After one of their visits, the agents would leave, but we would have to deal with the aftermath of the interview. I always had nightmares and flashbacks, but they were worse for several weeks after the FBI visits. Charlotte decided I could not and would not take anymore.

We found out years later after they stopped coming why they came so much. At the time they would not tell us anything, only that the interviews were necessary.

The reason they gave us at the time was that I was in so many different camps and might be able to help identify so many different people. We also learned they were writing a book to help the next men who would be POWs. It came in handy for the Vietnam guys. They set up a training camp in Colorado for the men to go through to teach them about POW camps. I understand some men only lasted seven days in the mock camp.

I was working on this book on January 12, 2006 and a friend of mine from the Pentagon called. He works for the Department of Defense. They were still trying to retrieve bodies from North Korea, and he wanted to talk to me about the battle of Onson.

We have a convention of Korean War Veterans, and my friend Phil O'Brien always comes, brings his maps, and talked to the men. I try to talk to Phil as much as I can because I am the only POW in the group and the man who was the farthest north. I do not feel like I am being "interrogated" by Phil like I was by the FBI, but I feel like I am helping him.

If the FBI had told me what they were looking for I might have been able to be of more help to them. While writing this book, we went through their records. They said I had a remarkable memory and came in contact with approximately 1500 men during my captivity. I had no idea I had seen so many. But I was in a lot of different camps, in different places, and working with the sick and wounded. I have to assume they are right. I see men now at the conventions who remember me that I do not know. I guess if there were that many I would not remember everyone. I only hope that somewhere along the line in the Hell Hole that we all lived through that something I did or said made one day or one hour easier for any one of them. I know some of my buddies said and did a lot of things that made a lot of days and hours easier on me.

If we had not stuck together, none of us would have survived to tell the story of the others who did not come back. My wife and I have been offered a trip back to Korea, but I never intend to go back. A lot of my friends have returned and really enjoyed themselves, but not me.

I came out of that place that was "hell on earth" to me and I have no intention of returning to it . . . Thank you, NO!

Chapter 15

Family At Last!

Joe Ascue and I had planned if we ever survived the time in prison we would meet and celebrate. My folks had moved to Chicago, and after my release from Oten, I was headed there to see them. I decided to take a side trip and stop in Bluefield and see Joe.

No one could have known when Dallas Mossman put my name on that list in Camp 2 in North Korea what kind of a journey he was setting my feet on.

After a long journey through North and South Korea, Japan, Guam, Hawaii, California, Texas, North Carolina, Washington D.C. and back to North Carolina, I would end up in Bluefield, West Virginia, to find a wonderful girl who would become my wife and would be the love of my life.

I was blessed with a great father-in-law and mother-in-law; no horror stories there. They treated me like family from the very beginning. I also have a wonderful son-in-law, Ralph Oakley, in Quincy, Illinois, who is a terrific provider and a good father to our granddaughters Allison Walker Oakley and Sullivan Smith Oakley.

Of course he could not have done that without the help of the best wife any man could ever have—our daughter, Lisa. She has been a great joy to her mother and me. When she and Ralph gave us Allison and Sullivan, it really was the ultimate gift. I have been allowed to watch my granddaughters grow from precious babies to mature young ladies. They are 21 and 19.

I don't know why I was spared when so many good men died, but I thank God every day for every day that I have. I try to live my life as a man who is thankful to be alive, and never take anything for granted, especially the love of family and the precious freedom we have.

The Celebration

I will tell you the story about Joe and me and the celebration we planned the entire time together in the prison camp. I don't think either of us really thought we would live to see the day we would go home, much less get together in the States, but it gave us something to talk about and look forward to, so we began to plan. We decided that we were going to "Pitch a drunk the likes of which a legend could be made."

We were both in trouble so much in camp and probably did as many foolish things for ourselves and others that it is a wonder we did survive. I look back now and I can't believe the guards didn't shoot me a hundred times over for all the things I did and said. I shudder sometimes at the stunts I pulled. Only by the grace of God did I get by with them. My wife points out to me that only the good die young. Joe and I certainly did not qualify for that honor in the prison camp.

When we came home, Joe was in better shape than I was, and he quickly married and started his family. He went to work and had a good life in Bluefield. I went to Walter Reed Medical Center for 14 months so our celebration had to be put on hold. I was on my way to Chicago to see my folks as I told you, when I made the detour to see Joe. I did not know it would be seven years before I ever made it to Chicago.

I got off of the Greyhound Bus. All I had was an address, so I took a cab. The cab stopped in front of a pretty, big white house on a quiet street. I got out, walked up the sidewalk, and knocked on the door. A small woman answered the door and told me Joe lived in the garage apartment at the back of the house and to go around the driveway.

It was August 15, 1955, another day that would really change my life forever. As with the first one in 1950, it happened so fast and so unexpectedly, but there I was in A MOMENT IN TIME.

I met Emily and Joey, Joe's wife and son. We came down the steps from the apartment and there in the backyard in the swing of the big house sat the prettiest girl I had seen in a long time. I noticed her dark blond hair and blue eyes. I guess I really was hooked from that day forward. I was introduced, and Joe and I left.

We decided to pitch our drunk. It lasted from Monday to Friday night when I ran out of money. We had gone through $326 and in 1955, that was a lot of money.

We got the "booze" and went to the city park where there was a water fountain. We sat there, talked, and drank until the booze was gone. We went after more and started over again. We didn't bother anyone, and no one bothered us.

We ran out of money and booze, and we went to Joe's house to face the first hurricane, Emily. Believe me this one was worse than any that would come after. Joe was so sick he went to bed. I did too, on Joe's couch on Friday night because I had very little cash left.

On Saturday morning, Joe was still sleeping so Emily and I had coffee. I figured I had better do something to try to calm the storm, so I rolled up my pant legs and started mopping the kitchen.

I looked up and there was the girl from the backyard. She had come to get Joey, the baby.

We asked Emily to go to the movie. We were trying to get on her good side. I took a chance and asked the girl if she would go with me and she said yes.

Now I will let her add her part of this story!

From Charlotte:

Everything he says is true, but there is more! I had been engaged off and on for two years while I was in high school and Business College. He turned out to be a real jerk. We broke up on Friday night. I was mad at everyone including God. I did not say my prayers on Friday or Saturday night. On Sunday night, I went to bed and I prayed, "God send me someone to love and someone who will love me."

Then Bill knocked on the front door, lost, on Monday morning. You will never convince me of anything else except that God brought him to me.

My mother was the one who answered the door that Monday morning. I was still in bed, and she came up the stairs and said, "Get up, there is the best looking young man you ever saw going around to Joe's." She had been through the last two years with me, and she just wanted me to meet a nice guy and be happy.

God brought me one of the truly nice guys of this world, and I could not have been happier. I have told so many friends that all I ever wanted was to be a wife and mother. Bill has given me that dream and so much more. He has given it to me with love, kindness, and generosity.

My generation always wanted a knight on a white horse in shining armor. Unfortunately, I guess we all have to go through the bad to get to the good. That day I went out to the swing as quickly as I could and sat down. Joe and the guy came out of the apartment, and Mom was right. He was something! Joe introduced me, and they left.

They were gone until Friday. When they came back, Emily was so mad, and I didn't blame her. They looked terrible. They went to the apartment and all heck broke loose. After a little while, everything was quiet. TOO QUIET.

On Saturday morning I decided I would go get Joey so if the fight broke out again, he would be out of it. Emily was taking care of Joey. She was seething, and I didn't blame her. Joe was asleep, and Bill was mopping the kitchen.

I figured maybe Bill was not all bad if he could help her clean up after he had helped make her so mad. When he looked up with those big black eyes, black curly hair, and bare feet, and asked me if I would go to the movies with him, how could I refuse?

We went to see Pete Kelly's Blues. We were walking down the street in front of the drugstore and my ex-fiancé stepped right out in our path. He nearly dropped dead. He had just told a friend, "Charlotte is probably sitting home, pining for me, with nothing better to do. I think I may give her a call. I have nothing better to do this weekend while I am home on leave."

Bill was holding my hand and was laughing and smiling at me, like he was having the time of his life. I simply smiled and said, "Hello, Russell." Bill and I kept walking, and I never looked back. I have never looked back. We were married December 24, 1955. We could not be happier. Bill is the love of my life.

We have one daughter, Lisa, and two granddaughters, Allison Walker Oakley and Sullivan Smith Oakley. The girls were both named for Bill—Walker and Smith—and along with Lisa and I, they have been the loves of his life. He has spoiled all four of us.

God answered my prayer for someone to love and someone to love me. I am sorry that Bill and Joe went though the hell of captivity, but if they hadn't, I would not have met him and my life would have been very different. I thank God for Bill every day!
—*Charlotte*

Friends

There are so many friends that have meant so much to us over the years. Ed and Mary Zeller, are so special to us and have always been such good friends and visited in our home. Ed is gone now, but Mary is still part of the family.

Martina Sparks, the widow of Jim Sparks of Bakersfield, California, and Pat Ruff, the widow of Will Ruff of Pell Lake Wisconsin. They are so close to us. I was in Camp 2 with both of these men. There were closer than brothers to me, and when they died, I really lost a part of myself. I hope these wonderful ladies will always be close to us because they are family.

If I tried to mention all of my buddies and their great wives, I would never finish this book.

I must take time to give credit to the wives of all EX-POWs. Without these terrific, dedicated women most of us would not have made it through the last 55 years. I know I would not. It is not just the men who were POWs, it is their entire family, because it changes our entire outlook on life and our personality and these women have learned how to make our lives better.

GOD BLESS YOU ALL!

POW HUSBANDS

Then came the tears
The nightmares
The kicking their wives out of bed
The startled reaction from a loud noise
The reaction from someone behind them
The opening of a door slowly and looking right
    and left before exiting
Not touching while asleep.

I took the good times
I'll take the bad times
I love you
JUST THE WAY YOU ARE
That's the way the wives of former prisoners of war
    have to live with our men—
JUST THE WAY THEY ARE!

So tormented with pain
So emotionally scarred
Still we love them
JUST THE WAY THEY ARE!

    —UNKNOWN POW WIFE

"Freedom has a taste to those who fought and almost died that the protected will never know."

—*Unknown POW Vietnam*

Afterword

I have been asked on more than one occasion if I ever have had "survivor's guilt." I would not call it guilt, but I can't help but wonder and question, "Why did I make it, and not the next guy?"

So many good men gave their lives for this country and the freedoms we have; so many died uselessly in the cold, and snow, and mire of those North Korean winters because

MAN'S INHUMANITY TO MAN IS UNBELIEVABLE.

We all ate the same food; we all slept in the same huts; we all did without a bath; we all endured the beatings, the solitary confinement, and the psychological trauma. Everything that one went through, we all went through together.

I have tried to live my life not only for myself and my family, but as a tribute to my friends who didn't come back and the ones that have passed away since we came home.

I am trying to teach the young people that I talk to, what happens when you don't learn from the past. Then it will only be repeated in the future. If I had my way, wars would end and all our young people would be safe. Nobody would have to fight another war again.

I have tried and tried to remember the time of the actual capture because this was the single event that changed my life forever, and when I look back I can only guess at the approximate time of day.

People say a moment can change your life and believe me that is true. I did not believe that was true until I was taken prisoner on that cold November morning in 1950. From that moment on, my life has never been the same and never will be.

I asked Dr. Pam Downing, my VA physician, and friend, "Will I ever be able to deal with this experience and be any better? Will the night sweats, the flash backs, the nightmares, the reactions to loud noises or being touched when I don't expect to be, ever be gone?"

She said, "No, if you did not have the reaction that you do I would be worried about you. What you went through was a life altering experience, and you will never be the same because your life was altered in a way few lives will ever be altered. Your reactions are very normal for this kind of experience, and the world should be proud of what you POWs did for us."

Endnotes

1 Michael J. Varhola, *Fire & Ice: The Korean War: 1950 - 1953* (Iowa, Savis Publishing Co., 2000), 245.
2 Andrew J. Birtle, *The Korean War, Years of Stalemate, July 1951- July 1953* (Virginia, U.S. Army Center of Military History, 2000), 36,
3 Birtle, 36.
4 Ibid.
5 Varhola, 245.

Bibliography

Birtle, Andrew J, *The Korean War, Years of Stalemate,
July 1951 – July 1953*, U.S.Department of Military History, 2000.

Varhola, Michael J., *Fire & Ice, The Korean War, 1950 – 1953*
Savas Publishing Co. 2000.

.

About the Author

William W. Smith was born in Bennettsville, South Carolina, and grew up in Rockingham, North Carolina, on a 1600-acre family produce farm. He was the second child of four born to Georgia Whittaker and Henry Boyd (H.B.) Smith.

He entered the Army for the first time in 1944 when he was only fifteen. When it was discovered he had lied about his age, he was sent home until he was able to reenter the Army in 1947. He was discharged in 1954.

He married Charlotte in Bluefield, West Virginia, in 1955. They have one daughter, Lisa, and two granddaughters, Allison Walker Oakley and Sullivan Smith Oakley. He and his wife currently reside in Quincy, Illinois, and enjoy traveling.

To contact the author and to obtain
more books, please write:

William Smith
2901 Broadway
P.O. Box 138
Quincy, Illinois 62301